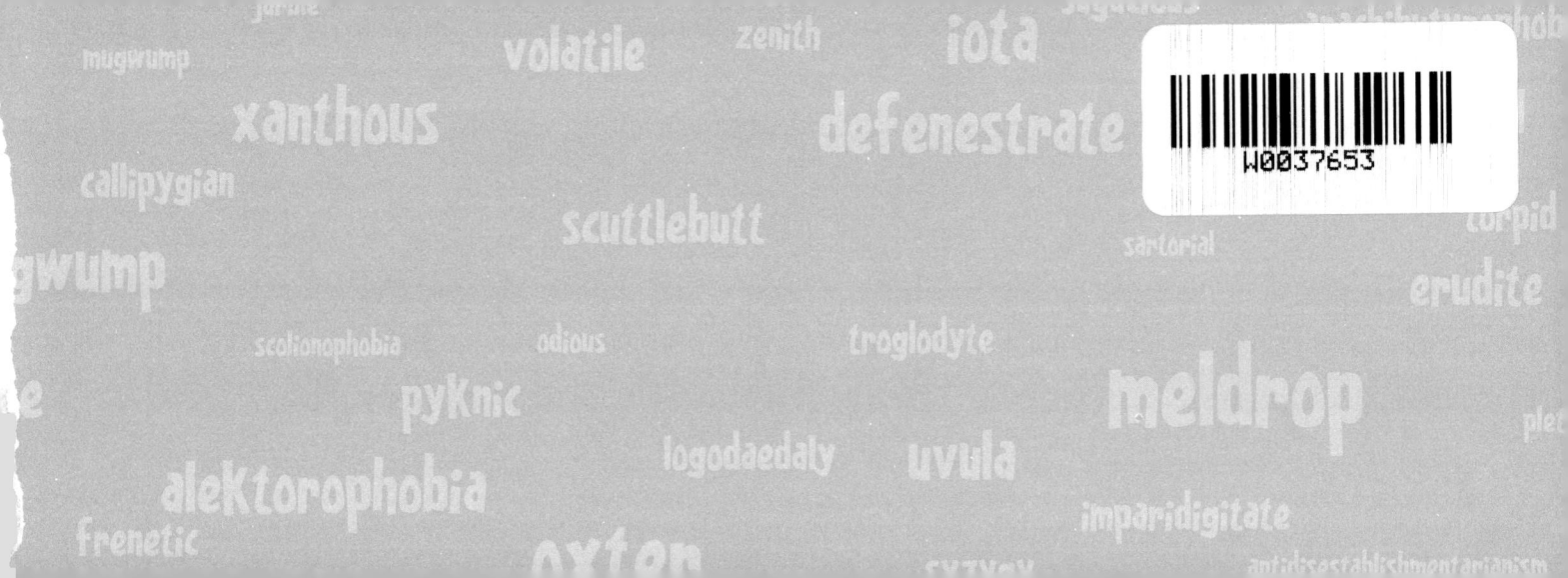

mugwump

volatile   zenith   iota

xanthous   defenestrate   W0037653

callipygian   torpid

scuttlebutt   sartorial

gwump   erudite

scotionophobia   odious   troglodyte

pyknic   meldrop   plet

logodaedaly   uvula

alektorophobia

frenetic   imparidigitate

oxter   syzygy   antidisestablishmontarianism

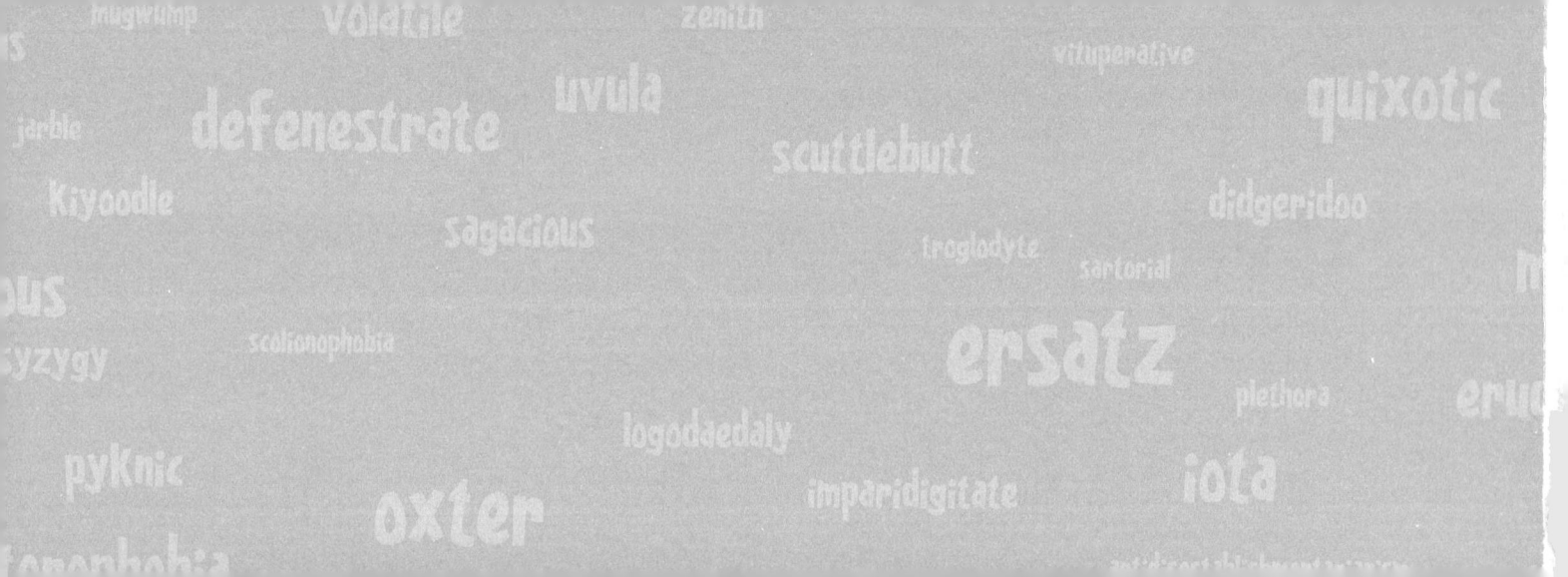

THE
SES·QUI·PE·DAL·IAN
DICTIONARY

illustrated by Marc Monés

innovative
KIDS®
Hands-On · Minds-On

A special thanks to the students of the Columbia Publishing Course whose initial concept led to the creation of this amazing, vocabulary-building game! To Lindy Hess for her unwavering out-of-the-box thinking and boundless energy and to Christopher Franceschelli for bringing us into the inner circle of the venerable Columbia Publishing Course.

TABLE OF CONTENTS

HOW TO PLAY THE SESQUIPEDALIAN WORD GAME

NUMBER OF PLAYERS

3 or more. (Groups of 6 or more may choose to break into teams.)

OBJECT

To be the first player to reach the *Egress*.

SET UP

- Place the game board in the middle of the playing area.
- Place the "sesquipedalian" minute timer in the middle of the playing area.
- Each player gets a pad and pencil.
- Each player chooses a pawn and places it on *Ingress*.
- Put *The Sesquipedalian Dictionary* to the side for easy access.

LET'S PLAY!

1. The player whose last name has the most letters goes first. Or, if there's more than one of you long-named lads or lasses, roll the die. The player with the highest roll starts the game.

2. Roll the die and advance the number of spaces indicated. Then complete the challenge noted on the space to earn bonus moves forward. (Rules for the different challenges and how many spaces forward to move are detailed below.) After the challenge is completed and any bonus moves are taken, the player's turn is over.

3. Each space on the board is color coded to correspond to a different challenge. To choose a word, players simply flip open *The Sesquipedalian Dictionary*. Whatever page the book opens to is the page from which players must select a word.

Draw It 🖉 The player chooses a word without telling other players what it is. (Look for this symbol 🖉 marking words that are easier to draw.) He or she then has one minute to draw a picture that illustrates the definition of the sesquipedalian word. The player cannot make any sounds or draw any letters, numbers, or symbols.

The other players try to guess the definition. (Correct guesses must be reasonably close to the way they are written in the dictionary but needn't be exact. For instance, if the definition for a word is "thin" and a player says "skinny," that should be considered close enough.) <u>Bonus Moves</u>: The first player to guess the word's definition gets to move forward one space. The player who drew gets to roll again and move forward the number of spaces indicated on the die. If no one guesses correctly, no one moves additional spaces forward.

For vocabulary-building play: The player may say the sesquipedalian word aloud before beginning to draw it.

Guess It The player chooses a word and reads it aloud to the other players. All the other players have one minute to write down what they think the word's definition is. They should fold their guesses in half before passing them in. Any player but the one whose turn it is may read the definitions aloud. The player who chose the word should guess who wrote each definition. <u>Bonus Moves</u>: The guessing player moves forward one space for each correct guess. Any player who wrote the correct definition of the word also moves forward one space. Any player who wasn't matched correctly to his or her definition gets to move forward one space.

Act It The player chooses a word without telling other players what it is. He or she has one minute to act out the definition of the sesquipedalian word without making any sounds. (Look for this symbol 🎭 marking words that are easier to act out.)

All other players have to try to guess the definition. (Again, definitions only need to be reasonably close to the way they are in the dictionary.) <u>Bonus Moves</u>: The first player to guess the word's definition moves forward one space. The player who acted gets to roll again and move forward the number of spaces indicated on the die. If no one guesses correctly, no one moves additional spaces forward.

For vocabulary-building play: The players can read the sesquipedalian word aloud before beginning to act it out.

Find It The player rolls the die again to select a corresponding chapter number in *The Sesquipedalian Dictionary*. Based on the title of that chapter, the player must pick which of the six words listed in the square on the game board belongs in that chapter. <u>Bonus Moves</u>: If the player guesses correctly, he or she gets to roll again and move forward the number of spaces indicated on the die.

Ad-Lib It The player chooses a word and tells the other players what it is. He or she writes down three definitions for the word—labeled A, B, and C—one of which must be the real definition. Each player has one minute to write down which definition (A, B, or C) is real. Players should reveal their guesses clockwise around the table from the player whose turn it is. <u>Bonus Moves</u>: The player who chose the word gets to move forward one space for each person he or she has tricked. (For example, the player has to define "Dodecahedron," and he says it means, "Definition A: something with 12 sides," "Definition B: something with 11 sides," or "Definition C: a type of elephant." If two people say "Definition B," two say "Definition C," and one says "Definition A," the player who chose the word moves forward four spaces.) Each player who correctly guesses the real definition moves forward one space.

Pick It The player may pick any challenge: Draw It, Guess It, Act It, or Ad-Lib It.

Expeditious Passage If a player lands on the space adjoining either Expeditious Passage, he or she may take this shortcut on his or her next turn. The Expeditious Passage square itself does not count as a space.

WINNING

Continue play clockwise. The first player to reach the *Egress* must pass the final challenge to win! The player in last place gets to pick any word from *The Sesquipedalian Dictionary*. (If two players are tied for last, they must work together to choose the word and craft the definition.) The player in last place then says a definition for that word, and the player at the *Egress* has to say if he or she thinks that the definition given is correct or incorrect. If the player's answer is wrong, then he or she must go back to the space labeled *Retrocede*. He or she continues play from there. If the player's answer is correct, he or she wins.

THE HOMEWORK CHALLENGE

Instead of using words from *The Sesquipedalian Dictionary*, use your vocabulary homework. The game play is the same, and it's a great way to learn words for school.

MORE FUN WITH WORDS

The Sesquipedalian Word Game will increase your vocabulary and boost your spelling abilities. Crossword puzzles, jumbles, and other word-based puzzles are also great vocabulary and spelling exercises. Read these next few pages for more fun ideas to help you build these skills.

HANGMAN

Hangman is a classic word game. You'll need a pencil, paper, and at least two players. Choose a word or phrase, and write down a number of blanks equal to the number of letters it has. For example, the phrase HAVE A BALL would be written out as:

— — — — — — — — —

Next, the other player(s) take turns guessing letters. A correctly guessed letter is written into the answer blanks every place it occurs

in the word or phrase. The player who guessed that letter gets to go again. Incorrect guesses should be noted at the bottom of the page.

If a player guesses a letter that does not appear in the word or phrase, the "man" starts to get hanged. The player who thought of the word or phrase draws part of the man onto a "gallows" with each incorrect guess. The parts are: head, body, left arm, right arm, left leg, and right leg. Add hands, feet, eyes, nose, and mouth to give players more chances to guess. Once a complete man has been drawn onto the gallows, the guessers have officially been stumped, and the player who thought of the word or phrase has won!

Want to try a truly sesquipedalian word? Write its letters scrambled below the blanks. Have players take turns guessing what the first letter of the word is, then the second letter, and so on. Incorrect guesses earn parts of the hangman. You can also play by writing the word without vowels.

GHOST

Another fun word game is Ghost, in which the object is to avoid being the player to complete a word. You'll need pencils, paper, and at least two players. (You can also play without writing.)

Start by having one player write down a letter. The next player thinks of a word that starts with that letter and adds its second letter. The next player then thinks of a word that starts with the two written letters and adds a third letter. Play continues until someone spells an entire word that is more than three letters long. The player who completes a word loses the round.

A sample round might go like this:
Player #1: T
Player #2: TR
Player #1: TRA
Player #2: TRAC
Player #1: TRACE . . . Since "trace" is a real word longer than three letters, Player #1 loses this round.

If you challenge the word your opponent is spelling, that player must then tell you the word he or she was thinking. If the word is real, the player who challenged loses the round; if the challenged player doesn't have a real word, then he or she loses the round. Each time a player loses a round, he or she earns a letter in the word "GHOST." The first player to earn all the letters in the word "GHOST" loses the game.

SESQUIPEDALIAN CATEGORIES

Categories is a game that involves thinking of words that begin with a certain letter. To give it a sesquipedalian twist, compete to see who can think of the longest word starting with a certain letter.

You will need pencils, paper, a deck of cards (without the jokers), and at least two players. To begin, each player draws a six-by-six grid and crosses out the upper left square. Then the players decide on a five-letter word with no repeating letters (such as "TWICE"). All players write this word down the first column on their grids. (Place one letter of the word in each box.) Shuffle the deck of cards, and turn the first five cards face up. Each card matches a category in the Category Chart. These categories are written across the top row of each grid.

Players then fill in each category of this grid with words that start with the letter at the beginning of the row. For example:

✕	Vegetables	Animals	Musical Instruments	Girls' Names	Games
T	turnip	tortoise	trombone	Tabitha	tic-tac-toe
W					
I					
C					
E					

After players have finished filling out their grids, see who thought of the longest words. One point is given for the longest word in each category. Ties get a point, too. The winner is the player with the most points.

x

A♠ Movies	A♣ Things That Are Cold	A♥ Body Parts	A♦ Girls' Names
2♠ Vegetables	2♣ Cities	2♥ Things That Are Red	2♦ Birds
3♠ Long Words	3♣ Things with Wheels	3♥ Last Names of Famous Actresses	3♦ Television Shows
4♠ Kinds of Fish	4♣ Desserts	4♥ Things That Are Loud	4♦ Drinks
5♠ Last Names of Famous Actors	5♣ Toys	5♥ Things That Are Flat	5♦ Things Made of Metal
6♠ Things That Move Fast	6♣ Musical groups	6♥ Things in a Woman's Pocketbook	6♦ Things Found Underwater
7♠ Things in an Office	7♣ Animals	7♥ Things You Plug In	7♦ Things That Are Blue
8♠ Things That Are Hot	8♣ Books	8♥ Things in the Room with You	8♦ Countries
9♠ Things You Can Wear	9♣ Things That Are Colorful	9♥ Things That Smell	9♦ Games
10♠ Song Titles	10♣ Things That Have Numbers	10♥ Things You Can Build With	10♦ Things in Outer Space
J♠ Musical Instruments	J♣ Things in a Kitchen	J♥ Boys' Names	J♦ Things That Take Batteries
Q♠ Things in a Garden	Q♣ Physical Descriptions	Q♥ Things You Use Every Day	Q♦ Things That Are Round
K♠ Things That Are Square	K♣ Things on a Farm	K♥ Things in a Classroom	K♦ Feelings and Moods

WORD SQUARES

A word square requires you to think of words that start with a pair of letters. This is a game for one player. All you need is a pencil and paper.

Begin by drawing a grid of any size, like the seven-by-seven grid at right. You will use it to write a clockwise spiral of words, beginning across the top row of the grid. The last two letters of each word must be used as the first two letters of the next word. For example, if your first word is SQUARE (see Square 1), your next word could be REMEMBER (see Square 2). A completed square (see Square 3) might read: SQUARE, REMEMBER, ERROR, ORPHAN, ANIMAL, ALPHABET, ETCETERA, RABBIT, ITALIC, ICEBERGS. Be careful not to choose a word which ends with two letters that a new word could not begin with. For example, your second word in the above example should not be RECORD.

To create a more sesquipedalian word square challenge, try to find the longest word possible that begins with the two letters of the preceding word. For example, if your first word was SQUARE, your next word could be REBARBATIVE. Consult *The Sesquipedalian Dictionary* to learn new words for your squares.

1.

S	Q	U	A	R	E	

2.

S	Q	U	A	R	E	M
						E
						M
						B
						E
						R

3.

S	Q	U	A	R	E	M
P	H	A	B	E	T	E
L	A	L	I	C	C	M
A	T	G	S	E	E	B
M	I	R	E	B	T	E
I	B	B	A	R	E	R
N	A	H	P	R	O	R

PRONUNCIATION KEY

a	apple, cat, happy	**ee**	clean, fiend, here, sweet	**ow**	house, how, our
ah	waffle, drop, sock	**eh**	head, pen	**oy**	boy, oil
air	tear there, fair	**er**	bird, hurry, learn	**uh**	duck, love, son, under, alone
ar	car, heart	**ahy**	fight, height, line, tire	**uss**	bus, fabulous
aw	all, law, talk	**ih**	big, finish, kit	**oo**	blue, food, soup
ay	day, fate	**oh**	no, hope, road	*oo*	look, put

MISCELLANY

A NOTE ON PRONUNCIATIONS

Recognizing and pronouncing fancy words in print is an important part of a good vocabulary. The pronunciations in this book are written phonetically. If you read the pronunciation just as it is written, you will pronounce the word correctly. Where a pronunciation contains a recognizable word, such as "deer" or "loot," read that word exactly as it is normally pronounced. When you pronounce the word, stress the part in capital letters. For example, the word *brouhaha* is pronounced: BROO-hah-hah. Stress the first syllable of the word. The pronunciation key shows how the vowel sounds are written out in the pronunciations. Give it a quick review, and you'll be on your way to sounding sesquipedalian in no time.

ABBREVIATIONS

These abbreviations are used within the dictionary:

adj.	adjective	*n.*	noun
adv.	adverb	*pl.*	plural
e.g.	for example	*sing.*	singular
interj.	interjection	*v.*	verb

USING THE CHAPTERS

Want a word for your brother who brags too much? Browse "Idiotic Insults and Captivating Compliments." Want a word for bragging? Try "Fancy Words for Regular Things." Need a word so long it will wow people? "Tongue Tanglers and Ticklers" is for you. Use these chapters and you'll be able to tell your brother that he's a *blitherskite* and you'd rather suffer from *pneumonoultramicroscopicsilicovolcanokoniosis* than have to listen to any more of his *jactancy*. Now that's something to brag about!

xvi

1
FANCY WORDS FOR REGULAR THINGS

(Words to Make You Sound Erudite)

abnormous, *adj.*
(ab-NOR-muss)
not normal; irregular
abnormity, *n.*

abomination, *n.*
(uh-BAH-muh-NAY-shuhn)
a shameful or disgusting thing; something that is despised
abominate, *v.*

abysmal, *adj.*
(uh-BIHZ-muhl)
immeasurably low; very bad
abysmally, *adv.*

ambiguous, *adj.*
(am-BIHG-yoo-uss)
having two or more possible meanings or interpretations
ambiguity, *n.*, **ambiguously,** *adv.*

ambivalence, *n.*
(am-BIH-vuh-luhns)
uncertainty caused by having conflicting feelings about something
ambivalent, *adj.*, **ambivalently,** *adv.*

antediluvian, *adj.*
(AN-tih-duh-LOO-vee-uhn)
extremely old-fashioned; referring to the long-distant past

antejentacular, *adj.*
(AN-tih-jehn-TAK-yuh-ler)
pre-breakfast

apathy, *n.*
(A-puhth-ee)
lack of enthusiasm or emotion
apathetic, *adj.*, **apathetically,** *adv.*

apoplectic, *adj.*
(A-puh-PLEHK-tihk)
furious or extremely angry; intense
enough to cause apoplexy (stroke)
apoplexy, *n.*, **apoplectically,** *adv.*

apoplectic

apropos, *adj.*
(a-pruh-POH)
appropriate; fitting; suitable

archaic, *adj.*
(ar-KAY-ihk)
old-fashioned; primitive; antiquated
archaically, *adv.*

auspicious, *adj.*
(aw-SPIH-shuss)
favorable; fortunate; promising
auspiciousness, *n.*, **auspiciously,** *adv.*

austere, *adj.*
(aw-STEER)
serious, severe, strict, or hard; lacking softness or decoration
austerity, *n.*, **austereness,** *n.*, **austerely,** *adv.*

avarice, *n.*
(AV-uh-rihs)
greed
avaricious, *adj.*

bailiwick, *n.*
(BAY-lih-wihk)
an area of skill or knowledge; field of expertise

baroque, *adj.*
(buh-ROHK)
excessive in ornamentation or detail; overly ornate; extravagantly complex; tacky
baroquely, *adv.*

behoove, *v.*
(bih-HOOV)
to be proper, necessary, or appropriate; to be beneficial or in one's best interests

benign, *adj.*
(bih-NAHYN)
kind or gentle; not harmful
benignly, *adv.*

brannigan

brannigan, *n.*
(BRAN-ih-guhn)
a noisy argument or fight

cacophonous, *adj.*
(kuh-KAW-fuh-nuss)
having a harsh, unpleasant sound
cacophonously, *adv.*, **cacophony,** *n.*

caliginous, *adj.*
(kuh-LIH-juh-nuss)
dim; dark; misty
caliginosity, *n.*
"Are you sure it's past sunset? It doesn't look **caliginous**
*enough out there," the vampire whimpered, peeking out
of his casket.*

camaraderie, *n.*
(kahm-RAH-duh-ree)
ease and goodwill among friends

candor, *n.*
(KAN-der)
honesty and frankness of expression; openness
candid, *adj.*, **candidly,** *adv.*

cathartic, *adj.*
(kuh-THAR-tihk)
cleansing or relieving; emotionally purging
catharsis, *n.*

cenatory, *adj.*
(SEHN-uh-tor-ee)
of or pertaining to dinner

chagrin, *n., v.*
(shuh-GRIHN)
1: a feeling of disappointment, humiliation, or mortification 2: to annoy via humiliation or disappointment
chagrined, *adj.*

chicanery, *n.*
(shih-KAYN-ree)
deception or trickery
chicane, *v.*

clandestine, *adj.*
(klan-DEHS-tihn)
secretive; furtive; sneaky
clandestineness, *n.*, **clandestinely,** *adv.*

coherent, *adj.*
(koh-HEER-uhnt)
connected by logic; logical
coherence, *n.*, **coherently,** *adv.*

6

conflagration, *n.*
(kahn-fluh-GRAY-shuhn)
a large and destructive fire
conflagrant, *adj.*

consuetudinary, *adj.*
(kahn-swih-TOO-duh-NER-ee)
customary; traditional
consuetude, *n.*

convoluted, *adj.*
(kahn-vuh-LOO-tihd)
complicated or intricate; twisted
convolutedness, *n.*, **convolutedly,** *adv.*, **convolute,** *v.*

copious, *adj.*
(KOH-pee-uss)
abundant; plentiful; in great quantity
copiousness, *n.*, **copiously,** *adv.*

coruscate, *v.*
(KOR-uh-skayt)
to sparkle or emit flashes of light
coruscation, *n.*

coulrophobia, *n.*
(kowl-ruh-FOH-bee-uh)
the fear of clowns
*Don't hire Bozo for Arnie's party unless you want to
activate the poor kid's* **coulrophobia!**

coup, *n.*
(koo)
1: a highly successful and unexpected act 2: a takeover

crepuscular, *adj.*
(kreh-PUH-skyuh-ler)
relating to or resembling twilight; dim
crepuscule, *n.*

cryptic, *adj.*
(KRIHP-tihk)
having mysterious or hidden meaning; puzzling
cryptically, *adv.*

delassation, *n.*
(dee-la-SAY-shuhn)
fatigue; tiredness

delectation, *n.*
(DEE-lehk-TAY-shuhn)
delight; enjoyment
delectable, *adj.,* **delectably,** *adv.*
There is only one news broadcast that brings sheer
delectation *to children, and it goes like this: "Due*
to heavy snowfall, schools will be closed today."

deleterious, *adj.*
(dehl-uh-TEER-ee-uss)
harmful; injurious to health
deleteriousness, *n.,* **deleteriously,** *adv.*

diaphanous, *adj.*
(dahy-AF-uh-nuss)
sheer; almost transparent
diaphanously, *adv.,* **diaphanousness,** *n.*

didactic, *adj.*
(dahy-DAK-tihk)
intended for instruction
didacticism, *n.*, **didactically,** *adv.*

dignotion, *n.*
(dihg-NOH-shuhn)
a distinguishing mark

discalced, *adj.*
(dihs-KALST)
barefoot
*It would have been impressive
if Lou had walked over hot
coals* **discalced.** *That he put oven
mitts on his feet seemed like cheating.*

discalced

discombobulated, *adj.*
(DIHS-kuhm-BAH-byoo-lay-tihd)
thrown into a state of confusion; confused; upset
discombobulate, *v.*, **discombobulation,** *n.*

discomfiture, *n.*
(dihs-KUHM-fih-cher)
state of being defeated, embarrassed, or ill at ease
discomfit, *v.*

disdain, *n., v.*
(dihs-DAYN)
1: scorn; a feeling of superiority 2: to consider others as
beneath oneself
disdainful, *adj.*, **disdainfully,** *adv.*

disparity, *n.*
(dih-SPAIR-ih-tee)
an inequality or difference
between things
disparate, *adj.*, **disparately,** *adv.*

draconian, *adj.*
(druh-KOH-nee-uhn)
excessively harsh, severe, or cruel

dubious, *adj.*
(DOO-bee-uss)
doubtful or unlikely
dubiousness, *n.*, **dubiously,** *adv.*

disparity

dysphoria, *n.*
(dihs-FOR-ee-uh)
a feeling of discontent, unhappiness, or depression
dysphoric, *adj.*

eccentricity, *n.*
(EHK-sehn-TRIH-suh-tee)
an oddness; a unique quality
eccentric, *adj.*, *n.*, **eccentrically,** *adv.*

eclectic, *adj.*, *n.*
(ih-KLEHK-tihk)
1: varied or mixed; comprised of things from different
sources 2: one who uses an eclectic method

edacious, *adj.*
(ih-DAY-shuss)
ravenous; extremely hungry
edacity, *n.*

effulgent, *adj.*
(ih-FUHL-juhnt)
shining; bright; radiant
effulgence, *n.*

egregious, *adj.*
(ih-GREE-juss)
extremely and obviously bad
egregiousness, *n.*, **egregiously,** *adv.*

eldritch, *adj.*
(EHL-drihch)
strange; eerie; spooky

elusive, *adj.*
(ee-LOO-sihv)
difficult to grasp or capture
elusiveness, *n.*, **elusively,** *adv.*

enmity, *n.*
(EHN-mih-tee)
deep-seated hatred or ill will
The **enmity** between the Mets and the Yankees is obvious
during any subway series.

ennui, *n.*
(ahn-WEE)
boredom; weariness

ephemeral, *adj.*
(ih-FEHM-uh-ruhl)
fleeting; short-lived

equanimity, *n.*
(ee-kwuh-NIH-muh-tee)
composure; calmness; stability of temperament

ersatz, *adj.*, *n.*
(ER-sahtz)
1: artificial; imitation 2: a lesser substitute

erstwhile, *adj.*
(ERST-wahyl)
former; previous

esoteric, *adj.*
(eh-suh-TAIR-ihk)
intended for or understood by only a particular group;
private; secret
esoterically, *adv.*, **esoterica,** *n.*

euphonious, *adj.*
(yoo-FOH-nee-uss)
pleasing or agreeable to the ear
euphony, *n.*, **euphoniousness,** *n.*, **euphoniously,** *adv.*

euphoria, *n.*
(yoo-FOR-ee-uh)
extreme happiness
euphoric, *adj.*
Hot fudge sundaes can
cause **euphoria** *in even*
the gloomiest of kids.

euterpean, *adj.*
(yoo-TER-pee-uhn)
pertaining to music

exigent, *adj.*
(EHK-sih-juhnt)
urgent; requiring immediate action
exigency, *n.*, **exigently,** *adv.*

euphoria

exiguous, *adj.*
(ihg-ZIHG-yoo-us)
meager; very limited in measure or amount
exiguously, *adv.*, **exiguousness,** *n.*

expeditious, *adj.*
(ehk-spuh-DIHSH-uss)
quick; speedy
expeditiously, *adv.*, **expeditiousness,** *n.*
"I'm in a hurry," said the snail to the boy. "It might be
more **expeditious** *if you carried me."*

facetious, *adj.*
(fuh-SEE-shuss)
not intended to be serious or literal; humorous
facetiousness, *n.*, **facetiously,** *adv.*

fallacious, *adj.*
(fuh-LAY-shuss)
false; misleading
fallacy, *n.*

farctate, *adj.*
(FARK-tayt)
stuffed; filled
    *"What's wrong?" asked Monique
when she saw Lyle lying on the floor and
groaning after Thankgiving dinner.
    "My stomach is so* **farctate**
*with food that I think it's
going to burst," said Lyle.*

farctate

fecund, *adj.*
(FEH-kuhnd)
fruitful; productive
fecundity, *n.*

feeze, *n.*
(feez)
a state of worry, anxiety, or fretful excitement; a tizzy

feral, *adj.*
(FEHR-uhl)
wild; untamed; not domesticated

fettle, *n.*
(FEH-tuhl)
one's mental or emotional state; mood

flabbergasted, *adj.*
(FLA-ber-gas-tihd)
to be utterly surprised or astonished
flabbergast, *v.*, **flabbergastingly,** *adv.*

flagitious, *adj.*
(fluh-JIH-shuss)
wicked; scandalous; shameful; highly improper
flagitiously, *adv.*, **flagitiousness,** *n.*

flagrant, *adj.*
(FLAY-gruhnt)
outrageously obvious or noticeable
flagrance, *n.*, **flagrantly,** *adv.*
The referees called a **flagrant** *foul after Lynn tackled Shana to the floor while Shana was dribbling the basketball.*

flavescent, *adj.*
(fluh-VEH-suhnt)
yellowish; becoming yellow

fortuitous, *adj.*
(for-TOO-ih-tuss)
happening by lucky accident or chance
fortuitousness, *n.*, **fortuity,** *n.*, **fortuitously,** *adv.*

foudroyant, *adj.*
(foo-DROY-uhnt)
stunning or dazzling in effect; striking
Ian's sequined tuxedo was so **foudroyant** *that the girls all called him "Lightning."*

frenetic, *adj.*
(fruh-NEH-tihk)
frenzied; frantic; wildly excited
freneticism, *n.*, **frenetically,** *adv.*

fritinancy, *n.*
(FRIH-tuh-nan-see)
a chirping or creaking sound

futile, *adj.*
(FYOO-tuhl)
ineffective or pointless
futility, *n.*, **futilely,** *adv.*

gratuitous, *adj.*
(gruh-TOO-ih-tuss)
1: given without charge or payment; free
2: unnecessary; without apparent reason
gratuitousness, *n.*, **gratuitously,** *adv.*

gulosity, *n.*
(gyoo-LAH-suh-tee)
an enormous appetite

hackneyed, *adj.*
(HAK-need)
overused or trite
hackney, *v.*

16

harbinger, *n.*
(HAR-bihn-jer)
something or someone that foretells of or indicates a future event

hebdomadal, *adj.*
(hehb-DAH-muh-duhl)
weekly
hebdomadally, *adv.,* **hebdomad,** *n.*

heinous, *adj.*
(HAY-nuss)
abominable; hateful; reprehensible
heinously, *adv.*

hypobulia, *n.*
(HAHY-poh-BYOO-lee-uh)
trouble making decisions
hypobulic, *adj.*

idiosyncratic, *adj.*
(IH-dee-oh-sihn-KRA-tihk)
peculiar; unique
idiosyncrasy, *n.,* **idiosyncratically,** *adv.*

ignominious, *adj.*
(IHG-nuh-MIH-nee-uss)
shameful; dishonorable
ignominiously, *adv.,* **ignominiousness,** *n.,* **ignominy,** *n.*

hypobulia

impecunious, *adj.*
(IHM-pih-KYOO-nee-uss)
lacking money; penniless; broke
impecuniosity, *n.*, **impecuniously,** *adv.*,
impecuniousness, *n.*

inconsequential, *adj.*
(ihn-kahn-sih-KWEHN-shuhl)
unimportant
inconsequentiality, *n.*, **inconsequentially,** *adv.*

incontrovertible, *adj.*
(ihn-kahn-truh-VER-tih-buhl)
undeniable; indisputable; not open to question
incontrovertibleness, *n.*, **incontrovertibly,** *adv.*

incumbent, *adj., n.*
(ihn-KUHM-behnt)
1: (followed by *upon* or *on*) obligatory; required
2: holder of an office
incumbently, *adv.*

inevitable, *adj.*
(ihn-EHV-ih-tuh-buhl)
unavoidable; certain
inevitability, *n.*, **inevitably,** *adv.*

innate, *adj.*
(ih-NAYT)
possessed at birth; inborn
innateness, *n.*, **innately,** *adv.*

innocuous, *adj.*
(ih-NAH-kyoo-uss)
harmless; safe
innocuously, *adv.*, **innocuousness,** *n.*

insalubrious, *adj.*
(IHN-suh-LOO-bree-uss)
unhealthy
insalubrity, *n.*

insipid, *adj.*
(ihn-SIH-pihd)
indistinct; uninteresting; bland
insipidness, *n.*, **insipidly,** *adv.*
Save your **insipid** *gossip for the next meeting of the TV Watchers' Union!*

insolence, *n.*
(IHN-suh-luhns)
rudeness
insolent, *adj.*, **insolently,** *adv.*

invidiousness, *n.*
(ihn-VIH-dee-uss-nehs)
creating jealousy, envy, or resentment
invidious, *adj.*, **invidiously,** *adv.*

iota, *n.*
(ahy-OH-tuh)
a tiny quantity
When Sam's mom saw that he'd gotten a D in English, she no longer cared one **iota** *about his A in math.*

irascible, *adj.*
(ih-RA-suh-buhl)
easily angered or prone to outbursts of temper;
temperamental
irascibility, *n.*, **irascibly,** *adv.*, **irascibleness,** *n.*

jactancy, *n.*
(JAK-tuhn-see)
boasting; bragging

jentacular, *adj.*
(jehn-TAK-yuh-ler)
pertaining to breakfast

jerkwater, *adj.*
(JERK-wah-ter)
insignificant; out-of-the-way

jobation, *n.*
(joh-BAY-shuhn)
a long and dreary scolding

lissome, *adj.*
(LIH-suhm)
flexible; supple
lissomeness, *n.*

lissome

lucid, *adj.*
(LOO-sihd)
1: intelligible; easily understood 2: clear of mind; rational or sane
lucidness, *n.*, **lucidly,** *adv.*

lugubrious, *adj.*
(luh-GOO-bree-uss)
mournful, dismal, gloomy, or sad, especially to an exaggerated degree
lugubriously, *adv.*, **lugubriousness,** *n.*

macabre, *adj.*
(muh-KAHB)
gruesome; horrifying; having death as a subject

malady, *n.*
(MAL-uh-dee)
a sickness

malaise, *n.*
(muh-LAYZ)
an unfocused or general feeling of being ill at ease or in discomfort

malfeasance, *n.*
(mal-FEE-zuhnts)
wrongful conduct, especially by a public official
Congressman Delray was accused of **malfeasance** *by the newspapers after they found out he had lied about his experience.*

malice, *n.*
(MA-lihs)
evil intention; ill will
malicious, *adj.*, **maliciously,** *adv.*

malleable, *adj.*
(MA-lee-uh-buhl)
capable of being shaped or influenced; adaptable
malleability, *n.*, **malleably,** *adv.*

malodorous, *adj.*
(mal-OH-duh-russ)
stinky
malodorously, *adv.*, **malodorousness,** *n.*

malodorous

mediocrity, *n.*
(mee-dee-AH-krih-tee)
state of being only of moderate or barely adequate quality
mediocre, *adj.*

melancholy, *n.*
(MEH-luhn-kah-lee)
sadness or depression; gloom
melancholically, *adv.*, **melancholiness,** *n.*,
melancholic, *adj.*

mellifluous, *adj.*
(meh-LIH-floo-uss)
smooth and sweetly flowing in sound
mellifluously, *adv.*, **mellifluousness,** *n.*

mendicant, *n.*
(MEHN-dih-kuhnt)
a beggar

minutiae, *n.*
(muh-NOO-shee-ahy)
small or minor details

morigerate, *adj.*
(mor-IH-jer-uht)
obedient
morigeration, *n.*

mucilaginous, *adj.*
(MYOO-suh-LA-juh-nuss)
sticky; soft; moist
mucilaginously, *adv.*

muculent, *adj.*
(MYOO-kyuh-luhnt)
moist and slimy

mundane, *adj.*
(muhn-DAYN)
unimaginative; dull; ordinary
mundaneness, *n.*, **mundanely,** *adv.*

nadir, *n.*
(NAY-der)
lowest point
When the lunch lady handed her the plate of mystery stew,
Sadie knew she had reached the **nadir** *of her day.*

nascent, *adj.*
(NA-suhnt)
emerging or just coming into existence
nascence, *n.*

nocent, *adj.*
(NOH-suhnt)
harmful, dangerous, or tending to cause injury

nonplussed, *adj.*
(nahn-PLUSST)
bewildered; completely perplexed or confused

nostomania, *n.*
(nah-stuh-MAY-nee-uh)
homesickness

nugatory, *adj.*
(NOO-guh-tor-ee)
insignificant; unimportant

nycthemeron, *n.*
(nihk-THEHM-uh-rahn)
a day and a night; twenty-four hours
nycthemeral, *adj.*

obsolete, *adj.*
(AHB-suh-LEET)
no longer used; outmoded
or old-fashioned
obsolescence, *n.*, **obsoletely,** *adv.*,
obsolesce, *v.*

obsolete

odious, *adj.*
(OH-dee-uss)
hateful; detestable
odiousness, *n.*, **odiously,** *adv.*

odoriferous, *adj.*
(OH-duh-RIH-fuh-russ)
smelly
*Even after opening the windows and turning on the fan, you only had to step into the room to know that Bart's **odoriferous** socks had been left there.*

oeillade, *n.*
(uh-YAHD)
a loving glance

ominous, *adj.*
(AH-muh-nuss)
foreshadowing something harmful or threatening; menacing; foreboding
ominousness, *n.*, **ominously,** *adv.*

onerous, *adj.*
(OH-ner-uss)
burdensome; troublesome; taxing

opsomania, *n.*
(AHP-suh-MAY-nee-uh)
an extreme longing for a particular food
*Today's **opsomania** is all about cheesecake; yesterday I could think of nothing but peanuts!*

ostentatiousness, *n.*
(AH-stuhn-TAY-shuss-nehs)
showiness
ostentatious, *adj.*, **ostentatiously,** *adv.*

pantophobia, *n.*
(PAN-tuh-FOH-bee-uh)
fear of everything
pantophobic, *adj.*, **pantophobe,** *n.*

penitence, *n.*
(PEHN-ih-tuhns)
state of being regretful for one's wrongdoing
penitent, *adj.*, **penitently,** *adv.*

penultimate, *adj.*
(pih-NUHL-tuh-miht)
next to last
penultimately, *adv.*, **penultima,** *n.*

penury, *n.*
(PEHN-yuh-ree)
a state of lacking money; poverty
penurious, *adj.*, **penuriously,** *adv.*

perspicaciousness, *n.*
(per-spih-KAY-shuss-nehs)
shrewdness; sharp perception or judgment
perspicacity, *n.*, **perspicaciously,** *adv.*, **perspicacious,** *adj.*

pervasive, *adj.*
(per-VAY-sihv)
spreading throughout; permeating
pervasiveness, *n.*, **pervasively,** *adv.*, **pervade,** *v.*

picayune, *adj.*
(pih-kee-YOON)
of little value or importance; trivial; petty

plethora, *n.*
(PLEH-thuh-ruh)
an overabundance or excess; a lot
plethoric, *adj.*
There's a **plethora** *of reasons that you're not going, but the most important one is that I said so.*

postprandial, *adj.*
(pohst-PRAN-dee-uhl)
occurring after a meal, especially dinner

pragmatic, *adj.*
(prag-MA-tihk)
practical
pragmatically, *adv.*

precipitation, *n.*
(prih-SIHP-ih-TAY-shuhn)
any form of water falling from
the atmosphere, such as snow,
rain, or hail
precipitate, *v.*

precipitation

precocious, *adj.*
(prih-KOH-shuss)
mature; advanced in development, aptitude, or ability
precociousness, *n.*, **precociously,** *adv.*

preposterous, *adj.*
(prih-PAHS-ter-uss)
absurd; foolish; ridiculous
preposterousness, *n.*, **preposterously,** *adv.*

primogeniture, *n.*
(PRAHY-moh-JEHN-uh-cher)
the state of being the firstborn or eldest child of the
same parents

propriety, *n.*
(pruh-PRAHY-uh-tee)
quality of behaving appropriately

prosaic, *adj.*
(proh-ZAY-ihk)
dull; commonplace; unimaginative
prosaicness, *n.*, **prosaically,** *adv.*

prudent, *adj.*
(PROO-duhnt)
sensible; wise
prudence, *n.*, **prudently,** *adv.*

pugnacious, *adj.*
(puhg-NAY-shuss)
quarrelsome, belligerent, or disagreeable
pugnaciousness, *n.*, **pugnaciously,** *adv.*, **pugnacity,** *n.*

punctiliousness, *n.*
(puhnk-TIH-lee-uss-nehs)
attention to minute details; precision
punctiliously, *adv.*, **punctilious,** *adj.*

quandary, *n.*
(KWAHN-dree)
a confusing or difficult situation; a dilemma

querulous, *adj.*
(KWER-uh-luss)
habitually full of complaints; whiny
querulously, *adv.*, **querulousness,** *n.*

quotidian, *adj.*
(kwoh-TIH-dee-uhn)
everyday; commonplace; recurring daily

rapaciousness, *n.*
(ruh-PAY-shuss-nehs)
greed
rapacious, *adj.*, **rapaciously,** *adv.*

rebarbative, *adj.*
(rih-BAR-buh-tihv)
tending to repel or irritate
rebarbatively, *adv.*

recalcitrant, *adj.*
(rih-KAL-suh-trihnt)
stubborn, resistant, or
disobedient
recalcitrance, *n.*
*Paul resisted for nearly two hours
before his father was able to drag
him into the bathtub. "You're
more* **recalcitrant** *than a
mule—and just as smelly!" his
exhausted father proclaimed.*

recalcitrant

redolent, *adj.*
(REH-duh-luhnt)
fragrant
redolence, *n.*

rendezvous, *n.*
(RAHN-day-voo)
a meeting at a particular place and time
rendezvous, *v.*

replete, *adj.*
(rih-PLEET)
(usually followed by *with*) filled or abundantly
supplied

rife, *adj.*
(rahyf)
plentiful; widespread

ruction, *n.*
(RUHK-shuhn)
a loud disturbance or argument; an uproar

ruse, *n.*
(rooz)
a clever trick, plan, or maneuver
Getting a sick day home from school called for a **ruse** *involving licked palms, make-up, and a light bulb.*

sagacious, *adj.*
(suh-GAY-shuss)
wise
sagaciously, *adv.,* **sagaciousness,** *n.*

saponaceous, *adj.*
(sap-uh-NAY-shuss)
soaplike; slippery
saponaceousness, *n.*

sartorial, *adj.*
(sar-TOR-ee-uhl)
pertaining to clothing or style of dress
If you're such a **sartorial** *expert, how could you wear such an outfit?*

FANCY WORDS FOR REGULAR THINGS

schadenfreude, *n.*
(SHAH-duhn-FROY-duh)
finding joy or satisfaction in other people's misfortunes

sebaceous, *adj.*
(sih-BAY-shuss)
secreting slime, fat, or grease; greasy

sedentary, *adj.*
(SEH-dehn-tair-ee)
1: staying in one place; settled 2: characterized by or accustomed to a great deal of sitting
sedentariness, *n.*, **sedentarily,** *adv.*

senectitude, *n.*
(sih-NEHK-tih-tood)
old age

serendipity, *n.*
(SER-ehn-DIH-puh-tee)
luck in making happy, unexpected discoveries; good fortune or luck
serendipitous, *adj.*, **serendipitously,** *adv.*

solecism, *n.*
(SOH-luh-sih-zuhm)
1: a social misstep or a breach of etiquette
2: a misuse of proper grammar

sophomoric, *adj.*
(sahf-MOR-ihk)
immature
sophomorically, *adv.*

soporific, *adj.*
(sah-puh-RIH-fihk)
inducing sleep; drowsy
soporiferousness, *n.*, **soporifically,**
adv.

supine, *adj.*
(SOO-pahyn)
lying on the back
supinely, *adv.*, **supineness,** *n.*,
supinate, *v.*

soporific

surreptitious, *adj.*
(ser-uhp-TIH-shuss)
sneaky, clandestine, or secretive
surreptitiousness, *n.*, **surreptitiously,** *adv.*

tempestuous, *adj.*
(tehm-PEHS-choo-wuss)
turbulent; rough; stormy
tempest, *n.*
This **tempestuous** *weather is going to destroy
my elegant hairdo.*

titillation, *n.*
(TIH-tuhl-AY-shuhn)
pleasant excitement
titillating, *adj.*, **titillate,** *v.*, **titillatingly,** *adv.*

torpid, *adj.*
(TOR-pihd)
sluggish; inactive; motionless
torpidity, *adj.*, **torpor,** *n.*

transient, *adj.*
(TRAN-zee-yuhnt)
lasting only a short time; fleeting; passing through
transience, *n.*, **transiently,** *adv.*

trenchant, *adj.*
(TREHN-chuhnt)
forceful or effective; sharp or caustic
trenchancy, *n.*, **trenchantly,** *adv.*

trepidation, *n.*
(TREH-puh-DAY-shuhn)
fear; apprehension; dread
trepidacious, *adj.*, **trepidaciously,** *adv*

truculent, *adj.*
(TRUH-kyuh-luhnt)
belligerent; defiantly aggressive or hostile
truculence, *n.*

ubiquitous, *adj.*
(yoo-BIH-kwuh-tuss)
everywhere at the same time; ever present
ubiquitously, *adv.*, **ubiquitousness,** *n.*,
ubiquity, *n.*

unscrupulous, *adj.*
(uhn-SKROO-pyuh-luss)
dishonorable; unprincipled;
immoral; crooked
unscrupulousness, *n.*, **unscrupulously,** *adv.*

Utopia, *n.*
(yoo-TOH-pee-uh)
a perfect place
Utopian, *adj.*

vespertine, *adj.*
(VEHS-per-tahyn)
of or relating to evening

vexatious

vexatious, *adj.*
(vehk-SAY-shuss)
troublesome; annoying
vexation, *n.*
*The flies were **vexatious** to Floyd, but Floyd's
swatting was **vexatious** to the flies.*

visceral, *adj.*
(VIH-suh-ruhl)
instinctive, as a gut reaction
viscera, *n.*

vituperative, *adj.*
(vahy-TOO-puh-ruh-tihv)
harshly or abusively critical; mean
vituperate, *v.*, **vituperator,** *n.*, **vituperatively,** *adv.*

volatile, *adj.*
(VAHL-uh-tuhl)
unstable; tending to change from one state or condition
to another; explosive
volatility, *n.*

voluminous, *adj.*
(vuh-LOO-muh-nuss)
large in size or quantity; filling its space
voluminousness, *n.,* **voluminously,** *adv.*

voracious, *adj.*
(vuh-RAY-shuss)
1: ravenously hungry 2: extremely eager to take
something in
voracity, *n.*

xanthous, *adj.*
(ZAN-thuss)
yellow or yellowish

zenith, *n.*
(ZEE-nuhth)
highest point
zenithal, *adj.*
My life of crime has reached its **zenith**. *I finally made
the ten-most-wanted list!*

36

2
TONGUE TANGLERS AND TICKLERS
(Words That Are Looong or Just Fun to Say)

acousticophobia, *n.*
(uh-KOO-stih-kuh-FOH-bee-uh)
the fear of noise
acousticophobic, *adj.*, **acousticophobe,** *n.*

aflunters, *adj.*
(uh-FLUHN-terz)
in a state of disorder; messy

agrizoophobia, *n.*
(ag-rih-ZOH-uh-FOH-bee-uh)
the fear of wild animals
agrizoophobic, *adj.*, **agrizoophobe,** *n.*

ailurophobia, *n.*
(ahy-LER-uh-FOH-bee-uh)
the fear of cats
ailurophobic, *adj.*, **ailurophobe,** *n.*

alektorophobia, *n.*
(uh-LEHK-ter-uh-FOH-bee-uh)
the fear of chickens
alektorophobic, *adj.*, **alektorophobe,** *n.*

"When did you have your first attack of
***alektorophobia?"** the doctor asked Max.*
*"Let's see," said Max. "It must have
been when that crazy chicken chased me
down the road!"*

alektorophobia

alopeciaphobia, *n.*
(a-loh-PEE-shuh-FOH-bee-uh)
the fear of balding
alopeciaphobic, *adj.*, **alopeciaphobe,** *n.*

antidisestablishmentarianism, *n.*
(AN-tee-dihs-uh-STAB-lihsh-muhn-TAIR-ee-uhn-ih-zuhm)
opposition to the belief that there should not be an official church in a country
antidisestablishmentarian, *n.*

antiquarianism, *n.*
(AN-tuh-KWAIR-ee-uhn-ih-zuhm)
the collecting of antiques
antiquarian, *n.*

aposiopesis, *n.*
(AP-uh-SAHY-uh-PEE-suss)
the breaking off in the middle of speaking a thought

arachibutyrophobia, *n.*
(uh-RAK-uh-byoo-TEER-uh-FOH-bee-uh)
a fear of peanut butter sticking to the roof of one's mouth
arachibutyrophobic, *adj.*, **arachibutyrophobe,** *n.*

attitudinarianism, *n.*
(A-tih-TOOD-uh-NAIR-ee-uhn-ih-zuhm)
the assuming of an attitude or posture for effect
Wearing sunglasses in class got Lee sent to the principal's office for **attitudinarianism,** *but his cool won him the admiration of his classmates.*

autodysomophobia, *n.*
(AW-toh-DIHS-soh-muh-FOH-bee-uh)
the fear that one has unpleasant body odor
autodysomophobic, *adj.*, **autodysomophobe,** *n.*

bafflegab, *n.*
(BA-fuhl-gab)
incomprehensible speech; nonsense

bamboozle, *v.*
(bam-BOO-zuhl)
to deceive by trickery
bamboozlement, *n.*

billabong, *n.*
(BIH-luh-bahng)
a pool of water found in an otherwise dry riverbed

blunderbuss, *n.*
(BLUHN-der-buss)
an insensitive, blundering person

boondoggle, *n.*
(BOON-dah-guhl)
a project that is a waste of time or money
Building an amusement park on Mars is a **boondoggle***; everyone knows Martians prefer traveling to Earth for fun.*

brouhaha, *n.*
(BROO-hah-hah)
an uproar

bubkes, *n.*
(BUHB-kihs)
nothing

cacospectamania, *n.*
(ka-kuh-SPEHK-tuh-MAY-nee-uh)
obsession with staring at anything
repulsive

camelopard

camelopard, *n.*
(kuh-MEHL-luh-pahrd)
a giraffe

cathisophobia, *n.*
(ka-THIHS-uh-FOH-bee-uh)
the fear of sitting
cathisophobic, *adj.*, **cathisophobe,** *n.*

**Chargoggagoggmanchauggagoggchaubuna-
gungamaugg,** *n.*
(It's pronounced just like it's spelled!)
name of a lake; longest place name in the United States

chrematophobia, *n.*
(kree-MAT-uh-FOH-bee-uh)
the fear of money
chrematophobic, *adj.,* **chrematophobe,** *n.*

clapperclaw, *v.*
(KLA-per-klaw)
to direct foul language toward someone

clodhopper, *n.*
(KLAHD-hah-per)
1: a clumsy, uncultured person;
a bumpkin 2: a big, heavy shoe
*While the other girls danced gracefully
in light, strappy sandals, Agnes
plodded around the dance floor in her* **clodhoppers**.

clodhoppers

codswallop, *n.*
(KAHDZ-wahl-uhp)
nonsense

collieshangie, *n.*
(KAH-lee-SHANG-ee)
a brawl

comiconomenclaturism, *n.*
(KAH-mihk-oh-NOH-muhn-KLAY-cher-ih-zuhm)
the collecting of funny names

diamerismapygian, *n.*
(dahy-AM-er-ihz-muh-PIH-jee-uhn)
one having a flattened buttocks
diamerismapygous, *adj.,* **diamerismapygia,** *n.*

42

didgeridoo, *n.*
(DIH-juh-ree-doo)
a large wooden musical instrument of Australian
Aboriginals

doddle, *n.*
(DAHD-uhl)
an easy task

donnybrook, *n.*
(DAH-nee-brook)
an uproar or brawl
*When the swimming pool was closed during the heat wave,
the kids banded together and caused a real* **donnybrook.**

entomophobia, *n.*
(EHN-tuh-muh-FOH-bee-uh)
the fear of bugs
entomophobic, *adj.*, **entomophobe,** *n.*

ergasiophobia, *n.*
(er-GAS-ee-oh-FOH-bee-uh)
the fear of work
ergasiophobic, *adj.*, **ergasiophobe,** *n.*

faffle, *v.*
(FAF-uhl)
to stammer
*Alex had a crush on Morgan, but when he saw her, all he
did was* **faffle.** *"H-h-hi," he said. "H-how are y-y-you
doing?" By the time the greeting was out of Alex's mouth,
Morgan was long gone.*

fandangle, *n.*
(fan-DANG-guhl)
1: an elaborate or fantastic
ornament 2: an act of silly behavior
or nonsense

fiddlesticks, *interj.*
(FIH-duhl-stihks)
an expression of annoyance

flapdoodle, *n.*
(FLAP-doo-duhl)
nonsense; foolish talk

fandangle

flibbertigibbet, *n.*
(FLIH-ber-tee-JIH-beht)
a frivolous, flighty, or silly person

floccinaucinihilipilification, *n.*
(FLAHK-see-NAW-see-nee-HIHL-ih-PIHL-ih-fih-KAY-shuhn)
deeming something worthless

flummery, *n.*
(FLUHM-uh-ree)
meaningless nonsense

fopdoodle, *n.*
(FAHP-doo-duhl)
a fool

frippery, *n.*
(FRIHP-uh-ree)
showy, fancy, or gaudy dress; trivial finery; fluff

frou-frou, *n.*
(FROO-froo)
frilly decoration

fysigunkus, *n.*
(FIH-sih-GUHN-kuss)
one who lacks curiosity

gadzooks, *interj.*
(gad-ZOOKS)
expression used to show surprise

galligaskins, *n.*
(gal-uh-GAS-kihnz)
loose pants that fall just below the knee (that were fashionable about 400 years ago)

galoot, *n.*
(guh-LOOT)
a clumsy or uncouth person

gardyloo, *interj.*
(gahr-dee-LOO)
"Beware of the water!" or "Look out below!"; warning cry used when throwing slops from the window into the street

gazump, *v.*
(guh-ZUHMP)
to rip someone off; to raise the price of
something after having accepted a lower offer

gewgaw, *n.*
(GYOO-gaw)
a showy trinket

gobbledygook, *n.*
(GAH-buhl-dee-GOOK)
incomprehensible speech; nonsense

gongoozler, *n.*
(gawn-GOOZ-ler)
one who idles by a canal; any idle spectator

guffaw, *n., v.*
(guh-FAW)
1. an uproarious burst of laughter
2. to laugh uproariously

haberdashery, *n.*
(HA-ber-DA-sher-ree)
men's clothes

hasenpfeffer, *n.*
(HAH-zehn-feh-fer)
a stew made from rabbit

hasenpfeffer

hemidemisemiquaver, *n.*
(HEH-mih-DEH-mih-SEH-mih-kway-ver)
a musical note played for an extremely short duration
(specifically, one sixty-fourth of the duration of a whole
note)

higgledy-piggledy, *adv.*
(HIH-guhl-dee PIH-guhl-dee)
in a confused manner

hippopotomonstrosesquipedaliophobia, *n.*
(HIH-puh-PAH-tuh-MAHN-struh-SEHS-kwuh-puh-
DAY-lee-uh-FOH-bee-uh)
a fear of long words
hippopotomonstrosesquipedaliophobic, *adj.*,
hippopotomonstrosesquipedaliophobe, *n.*

hobbledehoy, *n.*
(HAH-buhl-dih-HOY)
an awkward, gawky youth

hoi polloi, *n.*
(HOY puh-LOY)
common people; the masses

honeyfuggle, *v.*
(HUH-nee-FUH-guhl)
to deceive by flattery or sweet-talk; to swindle or cheat
I got the hall pass by flattering Mrs. Blackwell; a little
honeyfuggling *goes a long way.*

CHAPTER
2

honorificabilitudinitatibus, *n.*
(ah-noh-RIH-fihk-uh-BIHL-ih-
TOO-dih-nuh-TA-tih-buss)
a word invented by Shakespeare to
mean "the state of being able to
achieve honor"

hullabaloo, *n.*
(HUH-luh-buh-LOO)
a great noise, excitement, or
disturbance

humuhumunukunukuapuaa

humuhumunukunukuapuaa, *n.*
(HOO-moo-HOO-moo-NOO-koo-
NOO-koo-AH-poo-AH-ah)
a type of fish native to Hawaii; Hawaii's state
fish

   *When she got to the Big Island, her greeter
handed her a flowery lei, a hula skirt, and a little
fish in a bowl. "What's this?" she said of the fish.*
   "Why, it's a **humuhumunukunukuapuaa—**
our state fish," he said. "Aloha!"

hyperesthesia, *n.*
(HAHY-per-ehs-THEEZH-ee-uh)
acute and abnormal sensitivity to touch, pain, heat, or cold
hyperesthetic, *adj.*

hyperpolysyllabicsesquipedalianist, *n.*
(HAHY-per-PAH-lee-suh-LA-bihk-SEHS-kwuh-puh-DAYL-ee-uh-nihst)
someone who enjoys using really long words

hyperprosexia, *n.*
(HAHY-per-proh-ZEHK-see-uh)
a mental fixation on one idea

hypselotimophobia, *n.*
(hihp-SUH-luh-TIHM-uh-FOH-bee-uh)
the fear of high prices
hypselotimophobic, *adj.*, **hypselotimophobe,** *n.*

iatrophobia, *n.*
(ahy-A-truh-FOH-bee-uh)
the fear of going to the doctor
iatrophobic, *adj.*, **iatrophobe,** *n.*

ichthyophobia, *n.*
(IHK-thee-uh-FOH-bee-uh)
the fear of fish
ichthyophobic, *adj.*, **ichthyophobe,** *n.*

CHAPTER
2

imparidigitate, *adj.*
(IHM-par-ih-DIH-juh-tayt)
having an odd number of fingers or toes per limb
(1, 3, or 5)

infracaninophile, *n.*
(IHN-fruh-kuh-NIHN-uh-fahyl)
a champion of the underdog
infracaninophilia, *n.*

jobbernowl, *n.*
(JAH-ber-nowl)
a stupid person; a blockhead

kakorrhaphiophobia, *n.*
(kah-kawr-AF-ee-uh-FOH-bee-uh)
the fear of failure
kakorrhaphiophobic, *adj.*, **kakorrhaphiophobe,** *n.*

katzenjammer, *n.*
(KAT-suhn-JAM-mer)
a loud, unpleasant noise

kerfuffle, *n.*
(ker-FUH-fuhl)
disruption; commotion
There was a great **kerfuffle** *at the dog show when a trainer tried to put a tutu on a Great Dane.*

kiyoodle, *n.*
(kahy-YOO-duhl)
a mongrel or mutt (a dog of mixed or uncertain breed); a worthless dog
"The judges called my beautiful puppy a **kiyoodle***!" huffed Lauren, pointing at the walking furball by her feet. "But anyone with eyes can see she's a purebred Puffer-Snuffer."*

kiyoodle

lachanophobia, *n.*
(la-KAN-uh-FOH-bee-uh)
the fear of vegetables
lachanophobic, *adj.*, **lachanophobe,** *n.*

lollygag, *v.*
(LAH-lee-gag)
to move slowly or dawdle

misodoctakleidist, *n.*
(mahy-soh-DAHK-tuh-KLAHY-dihst)
one who hates practicing the piano

mugwump, *n.*
(MUHG-wuhmp)
a person who remains politically independent

mundungus, *n.*
(muhn-DUHNG-guss)
smelly tobacco

newfangled, *adj.*
(noo-FANG-guhld)
novel; new

niminy-piminy, *adj.*
(NIH-muh-nee PIH-muh-nee)
picky

mundungus

nincompoop, *n.*
(NIHN-kuhm-poop)
a fool or simpleton

ninnyhammer, *n.*
(NIH-nee-ha-mer)
a fool or simpleton
"Thanks," said Moe as he accepted two dollars for a fifty-cent trinket. "A **ninnyhammer** *and his money are soon parted."*

nonagenarian, *n.*
(NAH-nuh-juh-NAIR-ee-uhn)
a person in his or her nineties

octogenarian, *n.*
(AHK-tuh-juh-NAIR-ee-uhn)
a person in his or her eighties

olla podrida, *n.*
(OY-uh POH-dree-duh)
an assorted mixture; a famous Spanish stew with many ingredients
Jess invited jocks, computer nerds, cheerleaders, art geeks, and theater friends to her party. It was a real **olla podrida** *of personalities!*

osphresiophobia, *n.*
(ahs-FREE-zee-uh-FOH-bee-uh)
the fear of smells
osphresiophobic, *adj.*, **osphresiophobe,** *n.*

otorhinolaryngologist, *n.*
(OH-toh-RAHY-noh-LAYR-ihn-GAH-loh-jihst)
an ear, nose, and throat doctor
otorhinolaryngology, *n.*, **otorhinolaryngological,** *adj.*

panoply, *n.*
(PAN-uh-plee)
a grand array or display

paraskevidekatriaphobia, *n.*
(payr-uh-SKEE-vee-DEK-uh-tree-uh-FOH-bee-uh)
the fear of Friday the thirteenth
paraskevidekatriaphobic, *adj.*, **paraskevidekatriaphobe,** *n.*

peccadillo, *n.*
(peh-kuh-DIH-loh)
a small sin or fault

Pecksniffian, *adj.*
(pehk-SNIH-fee-uhn)
selfish or corrupt while acting kind; two-faced
Pecksniffery, *n.*, **Pecksniffianism,** *n.*

peenge, *v.*
(peenj)
to complain
*"If I hear you **peenge** one more time about school starting tomorrow, we're going to sign you up for weekend classes, too," Josh's mom warned.*

philotherianism, *n.*
(FIHL-uh-THEER-ee-uh-nih-zuhm)
the love of animals
philotherian, *n.*

pneumonoultramicroscopicsilicovolcanokoniosis, *n.*
(NOO-muh-no-UHL-truh-mahy-kroh-SKAH-pihk-SIH-lih-koh-vawl-KAY-noh-KOH-nee-OH-sihs)
supposedly the longest word in the dictionary; an artificial word claiming to mean lung disease caused by the inhalation of silica dust

pogonophobia, *n.*
(poh-GAH-nuh-FOH-bee-uh)
fear of beards
pogonophobic, *adj.*, **pogonophobe,** *n.*

poltroonery, *n.*
(pawl-TROO-nuh-ree)
cowardice

poppycock, *n.*
(PAH-pee-kahk)
nonsense

quackle, *v.*
(KWAK-uhl)
to choke or suffocate
*Tricia swallowed a fish bone and
started to* **quackle.** *Then she coughed, and the bone rocketed
across the restaurant and landed on a
stranger's plate.*

rhinotillexomania

rhinotillexomania, *n.*
(RAHY-noh-tih-LEHK-soh-MAY-nee-uh)
obsessive nose-picking
His **rhinotillexomania** *was so bad that when he ran
out of boogers in his own nose, he started sticking
his finger up other people's noses.*

rhombicosidodecahedron, *n.*
(RAHMB-ahy-KOH-sih-DOH-dehk-uh-HEE-druhn)
a geometric shape composed of sixty-two faces

scolionophobia, *n.*
(SKOH-lee-ah-nuh-FOH-bee-uh)
a fear of school
scolionophobic, *adj.*, **scolionophobe,** *n.*

CHAPTER
2

scuttlebutt, *n.*
(SKUH-tuhl-buht)
gossip; rumor

septuagenarian, *n.*
(SEHP-too-uh-juh-NAIR-ee-uhn)
a person in his or her seventies

shenanigan, *n.*
(shuh-NA-nih-guhn)
mischief; a prank

shivaree, *n.*
(shihv-uh-REE)
an elaborate, noisy celebration

skedaddle, *v.*
(skih-DA-duhl)
to leave quickly

skillygalee, *n.*
(SKIH-lih-guh-LEE)
thin, weak broth or oatmeal porridge

skookum, *adj.*
(SKOO-kuhm)
excellent; first rate; impressive

skedaddle

skullduggery, *n.*
(skuhl-DUHG-uh-ree)
clever trickery

slubberdegullion, *n.*
(SLUH-ber-dee-GUHL-yuhn)
a mean, low, despicable wretch; a rascal

snarf, *v.*
(snarf)
to eat or drink rapidly
"Mark, you don't need to **snarf** *your dinner," said Dad. "It's not a race!"*
"Oh, yes it is," replied Mark. "I'm trying to be the first one to get to dessert."

sniggle, *v.*
(SNIH-guhl)
to fish for eels

snollygoster, *n.*
(SNAH-lee-gah-ster)
a shrewdly unprincipled person; one who manipulates others for his or her own benefit

sockdolager, *n.*
(sahk-DAHL-uh-jer)
a deciding remark or knockdown blow

supercalifragilisticexpialidocious, *adj.*
(SOO-per-KA-luh-FRA-juh-LIH-stihk-EHKS-pee-AL-luh-DOH-shuss)
a nonsense word meaning fantastic

syzygy, *n.*
(SIH-zuh-jee)
the lining up of three celestial bodies

taradiddle, *n.*
(tahr-uh-DIH-duhl)
a fib; nonsense
Neal didn't consider himself a liar because he felt that **taradiddle** *didn't count.*

tchotchke, *n.*
(CHAHCH-kuh)
an inexpensive trinket

tohubohu, *n.*
(TOH-hoo-BOH-hoo)
a state of chaos; total confusion

tomfoolery, *n.*
(tahm-FOO-luh-ree)
playful or silly behavior
tomfool, *n.*

tomfoolery

trichotillomania, *n.*
(TRIHK-oh-TIHL-uh-MAY-nee-uh)
the compulsive pulling out of one's hair

triskaidekaphobia, *n.*
(TRIH-skuh-DEH-kuh-FOH-bee-uh)
fear of the number thirteen
triskaidekaphobic, *adj.*, **triskaidekaphobe,** *n.*

twee, *adj.*
(twee)
overly cute

twitterpated, *adj.*
(TWIH-ter-pay-tihd)
confused by affection; love-struck

ultracrepidarian, *adj.*
(UHL-truh-KREHP-ih-DAIR-ee-uhn)
beyond the scope of one's knowledge
ultracrepidarian, *n.*

valetudinarian, *n.*
(VAL-uh-TOO-duh-NAIR-ee-uhn)
one obsessively concerned with being sick

williwaw, *n.*
(WIHL-ee-WAW)
a violent storm rushing from the mountains to the sea; a sudden cold wind

WYSIWYG, *adj.*
(WIH-zee-wihg)
"**W**hat **y**ou **s**ee **i**s **w**hat **y**ou **g**et"
"Half the pieces of this puzzle are missing," I told the guy running the yard sale. "Where are the rest?"
"That's how it is at a yard sale," he said. "**WYSIWYG.**"

zenzizenzizenzic, *n.*
(ZEHN-zih-ZEHN-zih-ZEHN-zihk)
the eighth power of a number

zoosemiotics, *n.*
(ZOH-uh-SEE-mee-AH-tihks)
The language of animal communication or the study of such language

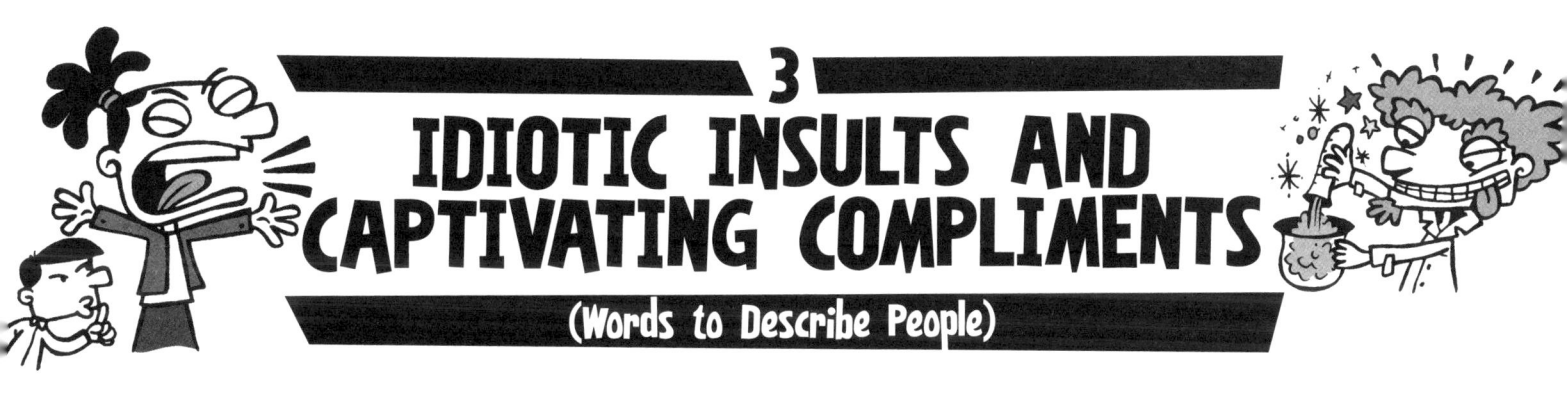

3

IDIOTIC INSULTS AND CAPTIVATING COMPLIMENTS

(Words to Describe People)

abderian, *adj.*
(ab-DEER-ee-uhn)
tending to laugh foolishly or constantly

accipitrine, *adj.*
(ak-SIH-puh-trihn)
hawklike
accipiter, *n.*

acerebral, *adj.*
(ay-SER-uh-bruhl)
brainless

adroit

adroit, *adj.*
(uh-DROYT)
skillful; nimble
*As the descendant of a long line of juggling tightrope walkers, Alison was the most **adroit** waitress in the restaurant.*

aesthete, *n.*
(EHS-theet)
a person who greatly admires beauty
aesthetic, *adj.*

affable, *adj.*
(AF-uh-buhl)
pleasant; friendly; approachable
affableness, *n.*, **affably,** *adv.*

agelast, *n.*
(AJ-uh-last)
one who never laughs

altitudinous, *adj.*
(AL-tuh-TOO-dih-nuss)
indefinitely high; tall

ambidextrous, *adj.*
(AM-bih-DEHK-struss)
able to use both hands with equal facility
ambidexterity, *n.*, **ambidextrously,** *adv.*

amenable, *adj.*
(uh-MEE-nuh-buhl)
agreeable
amenableness, *n.*, **amenably,** *adv.*

anserine, *adj.*
(AN-suh-rahyn)
gooselike

aquiline, *adj.*
(AK-wuh-lahyn)
curved like the beak of an eagle; of or like an eagle
Because he had an eagle eye for cheaters and an **aquiline**
nose, Professor Henry was known around campus as
the Eagle.

assiduous, *adj.*
(uh-SIHD-joo-uss)
hard-working; industrious
assiduousness, *n.*, **assiduously,** *adv.*

asthenic, *adj.*
(as-THEHN-ihk)
weak
asthenia, *n.*

astute, *adj.*
(uh-STOOT)
wise; shrewd; clever
astuteness, *n.*, **astutely,** *adv.*

audacious, *adj.*
(aw-DAY-shuss)
recklessly daring; spirited and bold
audaciously, *adv.*, **audaciousness,** *n.*, **audacity,** *n.*

bedraggled, *adj.*
(bih-DRAG-uhld)
soiled; messy

behemoth, *n.*
(buh-HEE-muhth)
something huge

beldam, *n.*
(BEHL-duhm)
an ugly, old woman; a hag

bedraggled

benevolent, *adj.*
(buh-NEH-vuh-luhnt)
characterized by goodwill, kindness, or generosity
benevolence, *n.*, **benevolently,** *adv.*

blatteroon, *n.*
(BLAT-uh-roon)
one who talks or brags constantly
blatter, *v.*

blitherskite, *n.*
(BLIH-ther-skahyt)
an annoying braggart

blunderbuss, *n.*
(BLUHN-der-buss)
an insensitive, blundering person

bogglish, *adj.*
(BAH-glihsh)
skittish; jumpy

bombastic, *adj.*
(bahm-BAS-tihk)
pompous or unnecessarily fancy in speech or writing
bombast, *n.*, **bombastically,** *adv.*

bon vivant, *n.*
(BAHN vee-VAHNT)
one who lives well and has refined tastes

bovine, *adj.*
(BOH-vahyn)
cowlike

Brobdingnagian, *adj.*
(BRAHB-deeng-NA-gee-uhn)
immense; enormous

brusque, *adj.*
(bruhsk)
rudely abrupt; gruff
brusqueness, *n.*, **brusquely,** *adv.*

bufoniform, *adj.*
(byoo-FAH-nih-form)
shaped like a toad

Bunyanesque, *adj.*
(buhn-yuh-NEHSK)
of astonishingly large size
Where the vase had fallen on his head, he had a lump of **Bunyanesque** *size—just like the ones they get in cartoons.*

Bunyanesque

butterfingers, *n.*
(BUH-ter-FIHNG-gerz)
a clumsy person
butterfingered, *adj.*

cadaverous, *adj.*
(kuh-DAV-russ)
emaciated; deathly thin
cadaverously, *adv.*, **cadaver,** *n.*

caitiff, *n., adj.*
(KAY-tihf)
a despicable and cowardly person

callow, *adj.*
(KAL-oh)
inexperienced; immature; lacking in adult judgment
callowness, *n.*

cantankerous, *adj.*
(kan-TANG-kuh-russ)
ill-tempered and quarrelsome; difficult
cantankerously, *adv.*, **cantankerousness,** *n.*

capricious, *adj.*
(kuh-PREE-shuss)
impulsive; flighty; unpredictable
capriciousness, *n.*, **caprice,** *n.*, **capriciously,** *adv.*

caustic, *adj.*
(KAW-stihk)
1: extremely sarcastic 2: harsh or corrosive
causticity, *n.*, **caustically,** *adv.*

cebocephalic, *adj.*
(SEE-boh-suh-FAL-ihk)
having a face like a monkey
cebocephaly, *n.*
*"Oh, my baby," said the mother orangutan. "How I love your tiny **cebocephalic** expressions! Show me mommy's favorite smile!"*

coiffure, *n.*
(kwah-FYOOR)
hairstyle
coiffured, *adj.*
*Lucy's bizarre new **coiffure** was the talk of the party. It had bangs, curls, bows, and little braids with beads.*

contemptuous, *adj.*
(kuhn-TEHMP-choo-uss)
haughty; scornful
contemptuousness, *n.*, **contempt,** *n.*,
contemptuously, *adv.*

coiffure

contumacious, *adj.*
(KAHN-too-MAY-shuss)
disobedient or rebellious
contumaciously, *adv.*, **contumacy,** *n.*
When Rob's mother got fed up with her conservative job, she became **contumacious** *by spiking her hair, getting a tattoo, and triple-piercing her nose.*

crony, *n.*
(KROH-nee)
a longtime friend

cullion, *n.*
(KUHL-yuhn)
a mean, vile man; a rascal

curmudgeonly, *adj.*
(ker-MUH-juhn-lee)
ill-tempered or cranky; full of resentment and bitterness; usually refers to an old man
curmudgeonliness, *n.*, **curmudgeon,** *n.*

dictatorial, *adj.*
(dihk-tuh-TOR-ee-uhl)
oppressively overbearing or domineering; of or like a dictator
dictator, *n.*, **dictatorially,** *adv.*

dilatory, *adj.*
(DIHL-uh-tor-ee)
tending to procrastinate or wait until the last minute
dilatoriness, *n.*, **dilatorily,** *adv.*

dilettante, *n.*
(DIHL-uh-tahnt)
one who merely dabbles in a field of knowledge; an amateur

diminutive, *adj.*
(duh-MIHN-yoo-tihv)
extremely small in size

disheveled, *adj.*
(dih-SHEHV-uhld)
unkempt, disordered, or sloppy, especially with regard to one's appearance
dishevel, *v.*

disingenuous, *adj.*
(dihs-ihn-JEHN-yoo-uss)
insincere
disingenuousness, *n.*, **disingenuously,** *adv.*

doddering, *adj.*
(DAH-der-ihng)
shaky or unsteady, as from old age
dodder, *v.*

doyenne, *n.*
(doy-YEHN)
the most respected or eldest female member of a group

ebullient, *adj.*
(eh-BOOL-yuhnt)
enthusiastic; bubbly
ebullience, *n.*, **ebulliently,** *adv.*

effusive, *adj.*
(ih-FYOO-sihv)
excessive in emotional expression; gushy
effusiveness, *n.*, **effusively,** *adv.*, **effuse,** *v.*

embonpoint, *n.*
(ahn-bohn-PWAHN)
chubbiness; the condition of being plump

enigma, *n.*
(eh-NIHG-muh)
one who is mysterious or puzzling
enigmatic, *adj.*, **enigmatically,** *adv.*

erudite, *adj.*
(ER-yuh-dahyt)
well educated
erudition, *n.*, **eruditely,** *adv.*

flaneur, *n.*
(flah-NER)
a loafer; one who shuns work

flibbertigibbet, *n.*
(FLIH-ber-tee-JIH-beht)
a frivolous, flighty, or silly person

flocculent, *adj.*
(FLAH-kyuh-luhnt)
fluffy or woolly
"He's okay," Kelly said, looking at Vic's short-haired beagle. "But I prefer that my pets be more **flocculent***," she added, pointing to her pet sheep.*

fopdoodle, *n.*
(FAHP-doo-duhl)
a fool

fractious, *adj.*
(FRAK-shuss)
quarrelsome; readily angered
fractiousness, *n.,* **fractiously,** *adv.*

frowzy, *adj.*
(FROW-zee)
unkempt; slovenly or messy; musty or bad-smelling

flocculent

gangling, *adj.*
(GANG-glihng)
awkwardly tall or long-limbed

gargantuan, *adj.*
(gar-GAN-choo-wuhn)
gigantic

garrulous, *adj.*
(GAIR-uh-luss)
extremely talkative
garrulity, *n.*, **garrulously,** *adv.*, **garrulousness,** *n.*

earance

geck, *n., v.*
(gehk)
1: one who is the object of scorn or is easily tricked
2: to dupe or to sucker

glabrous, *adj.*
(GLAY-bruss)
hairless
glabrousness, *n.*

gobemouche, *n.*
(GOHB-moosh)
a gullible person; a dupe or sucker

gracile, *adj.*
(GRA-suhl)
slender; graceful
gracility, *n.*

grizzled, *adj.*
(GRIH-zuhld)
partly gray or streaked with gray

grotesque, *adj.*
(groh-TEHSK)
extremely ugly and/or odd in ap|

guttersnipe, *n.*
(GUH-ter-snahyp)
a person of the lowest social class

haggard, *adj.* 🎭
(HAG-erd)
appearing worn or exhausted

harridan, *n.*
(HAIR-ih-dihn)
a bad-tempered woman

haughty, *adj.*
(HAW-tee)
arrogant and scornful of others; maintaining
an attitude of superiority; snobbish
haughtiness, *n.*, **haughtily,** *adv.*

highfalutin, *adj.* 🎭
(hahy-fuh-LOO-tihn)
pompous; snobby

hirsute

hircine, *adj.* ✏️
(HER-sahyn)
goatlike, especially in odor

hirsute, *adj.* ✏️
(HER-soot)
hairy
*When he finally came back home, he
hadn't shaved or cut his hair in weeks.
"You're as* **hirsute** *as a gorilla," his wife
said. "And just as smelly."*

hobbledehoy, *n.*
(HAH-buhl-dih-hoy)
an awkward, gawky youth
When the teenage delivery boy dropped another pizza, the pizzeria owner's wife shrieked at her husband, "Must you continue to hire **hobbledehoys***?"*

ignoramus, *n.* 🖉
(IHG-nuh-RAY-muss)
an ignorant person; a dunce

imperious, *adj.*
(ihm-PEER-ee-uss)
overbearing in an arrogant manner; bossy
imperiousness, *n.*, **imperiously,** *adv.*

imperturbable, *adj.*
(IHM-per-TER-buh-buhl)
unshakeably calm and collected
imperturbably, *adv.*, **imperturbability,** *n.*

incorrigible, *adj.*, *n.*
(ihn-KOR-ih-juh-buhl)
1: uncontrollable; willful; unruly 2: one who is unable to be reformed
incorrigibleness, *n.*, **incorrigibly,** *adv.*

indefatigable, *adj.*
(IHN-dih-FA-tih-guh-buhl)
tireless
indefatigability, *n.*, **indefatigableness,** *n.*, **indefatigably,** *adv.*

indolent, *adj.*
(IHN-duh-luhnt)
lazy
indolence, *n.*, **indolently,** *adv.*

ingrate, *n.*
(IHN-grayt)
one who is not grateful
ingratitude, *n.*

intrepid, *adj.*
(ihn-TREH-pihd)
fearless
intrepidness, *n.*, **intrepidly,** *adv.*

jehu, *n.*
(JEE-hyoo)
a fast driver
"Do you need to be such a jehu?" Dad asked Mom. "You're going to get another speeding ticket!"

jehu

jobbernowl, *n.*
(JAH-ber-nowl)
a stupid person; a blockhead

jocular, *adj.*
(JAH-kyuh-ler)
characterized by joking; given to joking

jowly, *adj.*
(JOW-lee)
having saggy flesh around the cheeks and jaws
jowl, *n.*

korinthenkacker, *n.*
(KOR-ihn-tehn-KUHK-er)
a person obsessed with trivial details

lackadaisical, *adj.*
(LA-kuh-DAY-zih-kuhl)
lacking enthusiasm; lazy
lackadaisically, *adv.*

laughingstock, *n.*
(LA-fihng-stahk)
the object of ridicule

Lilliputian, *adj.*
(LIH-luh-PYOO-shuhn)
extremely small; tiny

loquacious, *adj.*
(loh-KWAY-shuss)
very talkative
loquaciously, *adv.*, **loquaciousness,** *n.*, **loquacity,** *n.*

lucripetous, *adj.*
(loo-KRIHP-eh-tuss)
eager for gain; money hungry

lychnobite, *n.*
(LIHK-nuh-bayht)
one who works at night and sleeps during the day

maladroit, *adj.* 🎭
(ma-luh-DROYT)
clumsy

mammothrept, *n.*
(MAM-moh-threhpt)
a spoiled child

mattoid, *n.* 🎭
(MA-toyd)
a person who is semi-insane
"He's not a mad scientist yet,"
said the hunchback. "He's still
just a **mattoid** *at this point. But*
I'm sure he'll go completely crazy
soon enough."

mattoid

maverick, *n.*
(MAV-rihk)
one who takes a stand independently

mawkish, *adj.*
(MAW-kihsh)
overly sentimental
mawkishly, *adv.*, **mawkishness,** *n.*

mendacious, *adj.*
(mehn-DAY-shuss)
dishonest; lying
mendacity, *n.*

mensch, *n.*
(mehntsh)
an admirable, responsible, or generally good person

mercurial, *adj.*
(mer-KYOO-ree-uhl)
quick and changeable in mood; volatile
mercurially, *adv.*, **mercurialness,** *n.*

meticulous, *adj.*
(muh-TIHK-yuh-luss)
careful or precise with regard to details
meticulousness, *n.*, **meticulously,** *adv.*

micawber, *n.*
(mih-KAW-ber)
an eternal optimist

milquetoast, *n.*
(MIHLK-tohst)
a timid, meek, or fearful person

minuscule, *adj.*
(MIH-nuh-skyool)
tiny

misanthrope, *n.*
(MIH-suhn-throhp)
one who hates mankind
misanthropic, *adj.*

milquetoast

miser, *n.*
(MAHY-zer)
one who is selfish, greedy, or hoarding

mulish, *adj.*
(MYOO-lihsh)
stubborn
mulishness, *n.*

myrmidon, *n.*
(MER-muh-dahn)
one who obeys without question

mythomane, *n.*
(MIH-thuh-MAYN)
one prone to lying or exaggeration

naïve, *adj.*
(nahy-EEV)
inexperienced; unsophisticated; easily fooled
naïveté, *n.*, **naïvely,** *adv.*

nefarious, *adj.*
(nih-FAIR-ee-uss)
evil or extremely wicked
nefariously, *adv.*, **nefariousness,** *n.*

niminy-piminy, *adj.*
(NIH-muh-nee-PIH-muh-nee)
picky

nincompoop, *n.*
(NIHN-kuhm-poop)
a fool or simpleton

ninnyhammer, *n.*
(NIH-nee-ha-mer)
a fool or simpleton

numskull, *n.*
(NUHM-skuhl)
a stupid person; a nitwit
My sister is such a **numskull** *that she asked how much something cost in a dollar store.*

obdurate, *adj.*
(AHB-duh-riht)
stubborn or unyielding
obdurateness, *n.,* **obdurately,** *adv.*

obsequious, *adj.*
(uhb-SEE-kwee-uss)
fawning; overly eager to please
obsequiousness, *n.*

obstinate, *adj.*
(AHB-stuh-niht)
stubborn
obstinateness, *n.,* **obstinately,** *adv.*

obstreperous, *adj.*
(uhb-STREH-per-russ)
noisily and stubbornly defiant
obstreperously, *adv.*,
obstreperousness, *n.*

Kyle's little sister refused to go home, refused to put the extra books away, and refused to be quiet. When Kyle insisted, she threw a screaming tantrum in the middle of the library.

"You always pick the worst places to be **obstreperous**," Kyle groaned.

obstreperous

omnipotent, *adj.*
(ahm-NIH-puh-tihnt)
all-powerful
omnipotence, *n.*, **omnipotently,** *adv.*

ovine, *adj.*
(OH-vahyn)
of or like a sheep
ovine, *n.*

paisano, *n.*
(pahy-ZAH-noh)
a friend

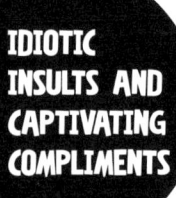

panjandrum, *n.*
(pan-JAN-druhm)
an important or pompous person

parsimonious, *adj.*
(par-sih-MOH-nee-uss)
cheap
parsimoniously, *adv.*, **parsimony,** *n.*

Pecksniffian, *adj.*
(pehk-SNIH-fee-uhn)
selfish or corrupt while acting kind; two-faced
Pecksniffery, *n.*, **Pecksniffianism,** *n.*

pediculous, *adj.*
(pih-DIH-kyuh-luss)
infested with lice
pediculosis, *n.*

petulant, *adj.*
(PEH-choo-luhnt)
unreasonably ill-tempered or irritable, especially with regard to some minor irritation
petulantly, *adv.*, **petulance,** *n.*

philosophaster, *n.*
(fih-LAH-suh-FAS-ter)
one who pretends to know more than he or she does

phlegmatic, *adj.*
(flehg-MA-tihk)
having a calm, slow temperament; not easily excited; unemotional
phlegmatically, *adv.*

pickthank, *n.*
(PIHK-thank)
one who flatters or gossips to gain favor

piebald, *adj.*
(PAHY-bawld)
spotted or blotchy

piebald

pilgarlic, *n.*
(pihl-GAR-lihk)
a bald-headed man

pinguid, *adj.*
(PIHN-gwihd)
fat and oily

pippin, *n.*
(PIH-puhn)
an admirable person or thing

poltroonery, *n.*
(pawl-TROO-nuh-ree)
cowardice
poltroon, *n., adj.*
*I'd never seen such a display of **poltroonery** as when Aaron's great big dog ran away from Maya's noisy but tiny Chihuahua.*

polymath, *n.*
(PAH-lee-math)
a person of great learning in several fields

pompous, *adj.*
(PAHM-puss)
vain and self-important

poltroonery

popinjay, *n.*
(PAH-puhn-jay)
a vain or conceited person

porcine, *adj.*
(POR-sahyn)
piglike

pretentious, *adj.*
(prih-TEHN-shuss)
showing off with the intent of attracting notice or impressing others
pretentiousness, *n.*

prodigious, *adj.*
(pruh-DIH-juss)
impressively great in size, force, or extent; enormous
prodigiously, *adv.*, **prodigiousness,** *n.*

puckish, *adj.*
(PUH-kihsh)
mischievous; playful in a naughty or annoying way
puckishness, *n.*, **puckishly,** *adv.*

pulchritudinous, *adj.*
(PUHL-kruh-TOOD-nuss)
beautiful
pulchritude, *n.*

pusillanimous, *adj.*
(PYOO-suh-LA-nuh-muss)
lacking courage; cowardly
pusillanimity, *n.*, **pusillanimously,** *adv.*

putrid, *adj.*
(PYOO-trihd)
rotten; foul-smelling
putridness, *n.*, **putridly,** *adv.*

pyknic, *adj.*
(PIHK-nihk)
short and fat

quiddler, *n.*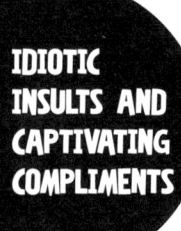
(KWIHD-ler)
one who wastes time

quidnunc, *n.*
(KWIHD-nuhnk)
a nosy person; a busybody

quixotic, *adj.*
(kwihk-SAH-tihk)
idealistic without regard to practicality; impulsive, especially for romantic reasons
quixotism, *n.*, **quixotry,** *n.*, **quixotical,** *adj.*, **quixotically,** *adv.*

rancorous, *adj.*
(RANG-ker-uss)
filled with resentment; hateful
rancor, *n.*, **rancorousness,** *n.*, **rancorously,** *adv.*

rapscallion, *n.*
(rap-SKAL-yuhn)
one who is playfully mischievous

reprehensible, *adj.*
(reh-prih-HEHN-sih-buhl)
deserving of blame
reprehensibleness, *n.*, **reprehensibly,** *adv.*, **reprehend,** *v.*

reticent, *adj.*
(REH-tih-sehnt)
reserved; not talkative; shy
reticence, *n.*, **reticently,** *adv.*

scabrous, *adj.*
(SKA-bruss)
rough
scabrously, *adv.*, **scabrousness,** *n.*

schnorrer, *n.*
(SHNOR-er)
a mooching person; someone who is always
borrowing

sinewy

sinewy, *adj.*
(SIHN-yoo-wee)
1: marked with defined muscle
connections 2: strong
sinew, *n.*
*I think superheroes only wear those tight
costumes to show off how* **sinewy** *they are.*

slubberdegullion, *n.*
(SLUH-ber-dee-GUHL-yuhn)
a mean, low, despicable wretch; a rascal

slugabed, *n.*
(SLUH-guh-behd)
a person who stays in bed out of laziness

smellfeast, *n.*
(SMEHL-feest)
a greedy freeloader; a moocher

snollygoster, *n.*
(SNAH-lee-gah-ster)
a shrewdly unprincipled person; one who manipulates others for his or her own benefit

stentorian

stentorian, *adj.*
(stehn-TOR-ee-uhn)
extremely loud
stentor, *n.*
   "Hey," Alisa yelled when she saw her friend, "come sit over here with me!"
   "Shhh!" the librarian hissed. "Your **stentorian** *ways are most inappropriate in here!"*

straitlaced, *adj.*
(STRAYT-layst)
strict in manners or opinion; extremely proper

struthious, *adj.*
(STROO-thee-uss)
ostrichlike

stumblebum, *n.*
(STUHM-buhl-buhm)
an incompetent, useless, or clumsy person

supercilious, *adj.*
(SOO-per-SIH-lee-uss)
disdainful; snobby; proud
superciliously, *adv.,* **superciliousness,** *n.*

superficial, *adj.*
(soo-per-FIH-shuhl)
shallow; concerned only with what is on the surface
superficialness, *n.,* **superficially,** *adv.*

swarthy, *adj.*
(SWAR-thee)
of dark color or complexion
swarthiness, *n.*

sycophant, *n.*
(SIHK-uh-fuhnt)
a fawning flatterer; a toady or lackey
sycophantic, *adj.*

taciturn, *adj.*
(TA-suh-tern)
habitually untalkative
taciturnity, *n.*

tenacious, *adj.*
(tih-NAY-shuss)
persistent; clinging
tenacity, *n.*, **tenaciously,** *adv.*

termagant, *n.*
(TER-muh-guhnt)
a violent or quarrelsome woman

thewy, *adj.*
(THYOO-wee)
muscular
thew, *n.*

timorous, *adj.*
(TIH-muh-russ)
full of apprehensiveness; timid
timorously, *adv.*, **timorousness,** *n.*
*The cat had fallen asleep waiting by the mouse hole
for the mouse to return. When the mouse got home, he
tiptoed in quietly, thinking, "Sometimes it is best to
be* **timorous**.*"*

troglodyte, *n.*
(TRAH-gluh-dahyt)
1: someone who lives in a cave 2: a person with extremely outdated ways or beliefs
*"If you weren't such a **troglodyte**, you'd know that you can download songs off the Internet now," the boy said to the newly thawed-out prehistoric man. "We've come a long way since you discovered fire."*

troglodyte

truttaceous, *adj.*
(truh-TAY-shuss)
troutlike in appearance

unctuous, *adj.*
(UHNK-choo-uss)
agreeable in an insincere self-serving way; oily; greasy; slick in nature; smarmy
unctuously, *adv.*, **unctuousness,** *n.*

unflappable, *adj.*
(uhn-FLAP-uh-buhl)
cool and collected; calm; not easily upset
unflappably, *adv.*, **unflappability,** *n.*

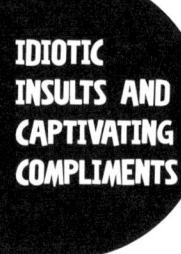

ungainly, *adj.*
(uhn-GAYN-lee)
lacking in grace; awkward

valetudinarian, *n.*
(VAL-uh-TOO-duh-NAIR-ee-uhn)
one obsessively concerned with being sick

vertiginous, *adj.*
(ver-TIH-juh-nuss)
tending to change for no reason; inconstant
vertiginously, *adv.*

vespertilian, *adj.*
(vehs-per-TIHL-ee-uhn)
batlike

wizened, *adj.*
(WIH-zuhnd)
dry and shriveled, usually due to old age
wizen, *v.*

wunderkind, *n.*
(VOON-der-kihnt)
one who achieves success or acclaim during youth

zaftig, *adj.*
(ZAHF-tihg)
pleasingly plump

4
PARTS, FARTS, AND FUNCTIONS

(Words That Have to Do with the Body)

ablutophobia, *n.*
(uh-BLOO-tuh-FOH-bee-uh)
the fear of bathing
ablutophobe, *n.*, **ablutophobic,** *adj.*

acrocephalic, *adj.*
(AK-ruh-seh-FAL-ihk)
pointy-headed
acrocephalia, *n.*

acronyx, *n.*
(uh-KRAHN-ihks)
an ingrown fingernail or toenail

agerasia, *n.*
(ag-uh-RAYZ-ee-uh)
the appearance of youth in an old person

akathisia, *n.*
(AK-uh-THIHZ-ee-uh)
a condition of extreme restlessness and incessant movement
akathisic, *adj.*

akimbo, *adj.*
(uh-KIHM-boh)
having a hand on the hip and an elbow bent outward

alopecia, *n.*
(al-uh-PEE-shuh)
baldness; hair loss
alopecic, *adj.*

anadipsic, *adj.*
(an-uh-DIHP-sihk)
extremely thirsty
anadipsia, *n.*
Even if I hadn't had a
drink of anything for days,
I don't think I would be
anadipsic *enough to drink*
out of the toilet—like my
dog does.

anadipsic

anconeal, *adj.*
(ang-KOH-nee-uhl)
pertaining to the elbow

anile, *adj.*
(AY-nahyl)
like an exceptionally old woman
anility, *n.*

autodysomophobia, *n.*
(AW-toh-DIH-soh-muh-FOH-bee-uh)
the fear that one has unpleasant body odor
autodysomophobe, *n.*, **autodysomophobic,** *adj.*

CHAPTER
4

97

bakerlegged, *adj.*
(BAY-ker-lehgd)
having legs that bend in at the knees; knock-kneed

benumbed, *adj.*
(bih-NUHMD)
to lose sensation or become numb, especially from cold
After she played in the snow all day, Keri's legs were so **benumbed** *that it felt like she had two tree trunks attached to her body.*

blennogenous, *adj.*
(BLEHN-ah-JEH-nuss)
producing mucus

blepharon, *n.*
(BLEHF-uh-rahn)
an eyelid
"Close your eye if you want to play hide-and-seek," Sara told the Cyclops. The creature's lone **blepharon** *slid down, but Sara still suspected he was peeking.*

borborygmus, *n.*
(BOR-buh-RIHG-muss)
gurgling or rumbling sounds from the intestines

brevirostrate, *adj.*
(BREHV-uh-RAHS-trayt)
having a short nose, bill, or beak

bruxomania, *n.*
(BRUHK-soh-MAY-nee-uh)
obsessive grinding of one's teeth

buccula, *n. sing.* **bucculae,** *pl.*
(buhk-yuh-LAHY)
fatty tissue under the chin; a double chin

callipygian, *adj.*
(ka-luh-PIH-jee-uhn)
having shapely or attractive buttocks

cerumen, *n.*
(ser-ROO-muhn)
earwax

cicatrix

cicatrix, *n. sing.* **cicatrices,** *pl.*
(SIH-kuh-trihks, SIH-kuh-TRAHY-sehz)
a scar
*Jim knew that people thought he'd gotten the
jagged **cicatrix** over his left eye from a fight.
In truth, he got it from falling off the jungle
gym as a kindergartner.*

coccyx, *n. sing.* **coccyges,** *pl.*
(KAHK-sihks, KAHK-suh-jeez)
the tailbone
coccygeal, *adj.*
*When Polly fell off the bunkbed onto her rear end, she was
lucky not to break her **coccyx**.*

coprolite, *n.*
(KAH-pruh-lahyt)
fossilized dung

coriaceous, *adj.*
(KOR-ee-AY-shuss)
leatherlike, especially with regard to skin

cowlick, *n.*
(KOW-lihk)
a tuft of hair that does not lie flat because it grows in a different direction than the rest of the hair

cowlick

crapulence, *n.*
(KRA-pyuh-lehns)
sickness caused by an excess of eating or drinking
crapulous, *adj.*

dactylion, *n. sing.,* **dactylia,** *pl.*
(dak-TIHL-ee-uhn, dak-TIHL-ee-uh)
the tip of the middle finger

dactylogram, *n.*
(dak-TIHL-uh-gram)
a fingerprint

dasypygal, *adj.*
(da-SIH-pahy-guhl)
having hairy buttocks
daspygous, *adj.*

diamerismapygian, *n.*
(dahy-AM-er-ihz-muh-PIH-jee-uhn)
one having a flattened buttocks
diamerismapygous, *adj.*, **diamerismapygia,** *n.*

diaphoresis, *n.*
(DAHY-uh-fuh-REE-suss)
sweat
diaphoretic, *adj.*

dolichocephalic, *adj.*
(DAHL-ihk-oh-suh-FAL-ihk)
having an unusually long head
dolichocephalous, *adj.*, **dolichocephaly,** *n.*

dolichoprosopic, *adj.*
(DAHL-ihk-oh-proh-SAH-pihk)
having an extremely long face

ectomorphic, *adj.*
(ehk-tuh-MOR-fihk)
having a thin body
ectomorph, *n.*

edentate, *adj.*
(ee-DEHN-tayt)
toothless
edentate, *n.*
The old vampire wasn't totally **edentate***; he still had a single fang that he brushed every dawn before going to bed.*

CHAPTER

4

effluvium, *n. sing.* **effluvia,** *pl.*
(eh-FLOO-vee-uhm, eh-FLOO-vee-uh)
foul-smelling fumes or vapor

emetophobia, *n.*
(ih-MEH-tuh-FOH-bee-uh)
fear of vomiting or vomit
emetophobe, *n.*, **emetophobic,** *adj.*
It was **emetophobia***, not fear of heights, that kept Liza from riding the roller coaster right after lunch.*

endomorphic, *adj.*
(ehn-duh-MOR-fihk)
having a heavy, round body
endomorphy, *n.*, **endomorph,** *n.*

epidermis, *n.*
(EH-puh-DER-muss)
skin
epidermal, *adj.*

eructation, *n.*
(ih-ruhk-TAY-shuhn)
a burp
eruct, *v.*

excrement, *n.*
(EHK-skruh-muhnt)
dung
excremental, *adj.*, **excrementitious,** *adj.*

expectorate, *v.*
(ihk-SPEHK-tuh-rayt)
to spit
expectoration, *n.*

fernticle, *n.*
(FERN-tih-kuhl)
a freckle

flatulence, *n.*
(FLA-chuh-lehns)
an excess of gas in the digestive tract
flatulent, *adj.*

expectorate

frisson, *n.*
(free-SOHN)
a shudder

furuncle, *n.*
(FYER-uhn-kuhl)
a boil; a pimple
furunculosis, *n.*

gargalesthesia, *n.*
(GAR-guhl-uss-THEEZH-yuh)
the sensation felt when one is tickled; the response
to being tickled
gargalesthetic, *adj.*

CHAPTER
4

gound, *n.*
(gownd)
the matter that collects in the corners of the eyes during sleep

hallux, *n. sing.* **halluces**, *pl.*
(HAL-uhks, HAL-uh-seez)
the big toe

hirci, *n. pl.* **hircus**, *sing.*
(HER-sahy, HER-kuss)
the hairs of the armpit

horripilation, *n.*
(HAWR-ih-puh-LAY-shuhn)
goose bumps
horripilate, *v.*

humerus, *n.*
(HYOO-muh-russ)
the upper-arm bone
humeral, *adj.*

hypnagogic, *adj.*
(HIHP-nuh-GAH-jihk)
of or pertaining to drowsiness; sleep-inducing

imparidigitate, *adj.*
(IHM-par-ih-DIH-juh-tayt)
having an odd number of fingers or toes
per limb (1, 3, or 5)

jubate, *adj.*
(JOO-bayt)
covered or fringed with long
hair; having a mane
like a horse

kyphotic, *adj.*
(kahy-FAH-tihk)
humpbacked
kyphosis, *n.*

jubate

labrose, *adj.*
(LAY-brohs)
having large or thick lips

leptorrhinian, *adj.*
(LEHP-toh-RIHN-ee-uhn)
having a long, narrow nose

macrosmatic, *adj.*
(MAK-rahz-MAT-ihk)
having a highly developed sense of smell

malacodermous, *adj.*
(MAL-uh-koh-DER-muss)
having soft skin

CHAPTER

4

105

masticate, *v.*
(MAS-tuh-kayt)
to chew
mastication, *n.*, **masticator,** *n.*, **masticatory,** *adj.*

meldrop, *n.*
(MEHL-drahp)
a drop of liquid suspended
from the nose
*After Dirk finally came inside,
drops of snow had melted from
the tips of his eyelashes. He had
to get a tissue to clean off a*
meldrop—*which may or may
not have been melted snow.*

meldrop

mesomorphic, *adj.*
(mehz-uh-MOR-fihk)
having a heavily built, muscular body
mesomorph, *n.*

mucopurulent, *adj.*
(MYOO-koh-PYER-uh-luhnt)
composed of mucus and pus
mucopurulence, *n.*

nutation, *n.*
(noo-TAY-shuhn)
an involuntary or spasmodic nodding of the head
*When Ashley's dad tries to fight off falling asleep in
front of the television, he exhibits more* **nutation** *than a
bobble head doll.*

**PARTS,
FARTS, AND
FUNCTIONS**

obdormition, *n.*
(AHB-dawr-MIH-shuhn)
tingling sensation and numbness ("falling asleep")
in an extremity due to pressure

obmutescence, *n.*
(ahb-myoo-TEHS-uhnts)
the loss of the ability to speak; the act of maintaining
silence
obmutescent, *adj.*

odontalgia, *n.*
(oh-dahn-TAHL-juh)
a toothache
odontalgic, *adj.*

olecranon, *n.*
(oh-LEHK-ruh-nahn)
the point of the elbow
olecranal, *adj.*

oneiric, *adj.*
(oh-NAHY-rihk)
having to do with dreams
oneirically, *adj.*
*Rita had such an **oneiric** experience that after she woke up,
she looked out her window expecting her pet unicorn
to be there.*

onychophagy, *n.*
(AH-nih-KAHF-uh-jee)
the habit of fingernail biting
onychophagus, *adj.*

oscitancy, *n.*
(AH-sih-tuhn-see)
1: the act of yawning 2: drowsiness
oscitant, *adj.*

oxter, *n.*
(AHK-ster)
an armpit
Steve knows how to make great fart sounds with his **oxter***.*

oxyosphresia, *n.*
(AHK-see-ahs-FREE-zee-uh)
an acute sensitivity to smells
oxyosphresic, *adj.*

oxter

pandiculate, *v.*
(pan-DIH-kyuh-layt)
to stretch, especially while yawning
pandiculation, *n.*

parorexia, *n.*
(PAIR-uh-REHK-see-uh)
the abnormal craving for items not suitable for consumption

parosmia, *n.*
(puh-RAHZ-mee-uh)
a disorder in which one smells odors that are not there
parosmic, *adj.*

pate, *n.*
(payt)
top of the head (usually refers to baldness)

phalanges, *n. pl.* **phalanx**, *sing.*
(fuh-LAN-jeez, FAY-lanks)
a finger or toe bone
phalangeal, *adj.*

phaneromania, *n.*
(FAN-er-uh-MAY-nee-uh)
the act of compulsively picking at scabs or other bodily
growths, including fingernails
phaneromaniac, *n.*

philtrum, *n. sing.* **philtra**, *pl.*
(FIHL-truhm, FIHL-truh)
the vertical groove at the center of the upper lip

pigeon-toed, *adj.*
(PIH-juhn-tohd)
having feet that point inward

platyopic, *adj.*
(pla-tee-AHP-ihk)
having a wide face

popliteal, *adj.*
(pah-pluh-TEE-uhl)
located at the back of the knee

proboscis, *n.*
(pruh-BAHS-kuss)
1: an elongated snout, like the trunk of an elephant
2: a long or prominent human nose

regurgitate, *v.*
(ree-GER-juh-tayt)
to vomit
regurgitation, *n.*

scatological, *adj.*
(SKA-tuhl-AH-jih-kuhl)
having to do with excrement or other bodily functions
scatology, *n.*

somnambulate, *v.*
(sahm-NAM-byoo-layt)
to sleepwalk
somnambulant, *adj.*, **somnambulation,** *n.*,
somnambulism, *n.*, **somnambulist,** *n.*,
somnambulistically, *adv.*

steatopygian, *adj.*
(stee-AT-uh-PIH-jee-uhn)
having large buttocks
steatopygous, *adj.,* **steatopygia,** *n.*

sternutation, *n.*
(STER-nyuh-TAY-shuhn)
the act of sneezing; a sneeze

suppurate, *v.*
(SUH-pyuh-rayt)
to form pus; to discharge pus
suppuration, *n.,* **suppurative,** *adj.*

tragus, *n. sing.* **tragi,** *pl.*
(TRAY-guss, TRAY-gahy)
the projection of skin in front of the opening to the ear

transudation, *n.*
(TRAN-soo-DAY-shuhn)
the act of sweating
transude, *v.*

uvula, *n.*
(YOO-vyuh-luh)
the small fleshy lobe that hangs at
the back of the throat
uvular, *adj.*
Imelda opens her mouth so widely
when she sings that I can see her
tongue, her tonsils, and her
dangling **uvula***.*

valgus, *adj.*
(VAL-guss)
bowlegged

uvula

vibrissa, *n. sing.* **vibrassae**, *pl.*
(vahy-BRIH-suh, vahy-BRIH-see)
whiskers

viscera, *n. pl.* **viscus**, *sing.*
(VIH-suh-ruh, VIHS-kuss)
the abdominal organs; intestines; guts
visceral, *adj.*

wattle, *n.*
(WAH-tuhl)
fleshy skin hanging from the neck or throat
(as of a bird)
wattled, *adj.*

xanthodont, *n.*
(ZAN-thuh-dahnt)
one who has yellow teeth
xanthodontous, *adj.*
Dwayne was such a **xanthodont** *that his smile looked like a fresh-cooked ear of corn.*

5
ASTONISHING ACTIONS
(Words for Things You Can Do)

ablution, *n.*
(uh-BLOO-shuhn)
washing oneself, especially as a religious ritual

abscond, *v.*
(ab-SKAHND)
to leave in a hurry

absquatulate, *v.*
(ab-SKWAH-chuh-layt)
to leave in a hurry

accubation, *n.*
(ak-yoo-BAY-shuhn)
the act of reclining while eating

alienate, *v.*
(AYL-yuh-nayt)
to turn away from someone to the point of making him or her indifferent or unfriendly; to estrange
alienation, *n.*, **alienated,** *adj.*, **alienator,** *n.*

ameliorate, *v.*
(uh-MEEL-yuh-rayt)
to make better; to improve
amelioration, *n.*, **ameliorative,** *adj.*, **ameliorator,** *n.*, **amelioratory,** *adj.*

amok, *adv.*
(uh-MUHK)
out of control; in a frenzy

apricate, *v.*
(AP-rih-kayt)
to bask in the sun

arietate, *v.*
(AHR-ee-eh-tayt)
to butt like a ram

assimilate, *v.*
(uh-SIHM-uh-layt)
to conform, adapt, or adjust; to make similar
assimilation, *n.*, **assimilated,** *adj.*, **assimilator,** *n.*

balbutiate, *v.*
(bal-BYOO-shee-ayt)
to stutter or stammer

bamboozle, *v.*
(bam-BOO-zuhl)
to deceive by trickery
bamboozlement, *n.*

bedizen, *v.*
(bih-DAHY-zuhn)
to dress or adorn in a showy manner
bedizenment, *n.*
*On her first day of kindergarten, Cynthia's mother let her pick her own outfit, unaware that she would **bedizen** herself in an old sequined gown and rhinestone jewelry.*

bedizen

beleaguered, *adj.*
(bih-LEE-gerd)
pestered, harassed, or badgered
beleaguer, *v.*

bespawl, *v.*
(bih-SPAWL)
to contaminate something by spitting on it

bloviate, *v.*
(BLOH-vee-ayt)
to speak or write over-elaborately or pompously

bombinate, *v.*
(BAHM-buh-nayt)
to buzz, hum, or drone
bombination, *n.*

brachiate, *v.*
(BRAY-kee-ayt)
to swing forward from handhold to handhold, using alternating arms, like a monkey
brachiation, *n.*
Billy's little arms were so strong that he could **brachiate** *his way from one side of the rope course all the way to the other.*

brachiate

cachinnate, *v.*
(KA-kuh-nayt)
to laugh very loud and hard
cachinnation, *n.*

cadge, *v.*
(kaj)
to beg, borrow, or impose
cadger, *n.*

calamistration, *n.*
(KAL-uh-mihs-TRAY-shuhn)
the act of curling hair

cancatervate, *v.*
(kan-KAT-er-vayt)
to heap or pile

canoodle, *v.*
(kuh-NOO-duhl)
to kiss and cuddle

clapperclaw, *v.*
(KLA-per-klaw)
to direct foul language toward someone
"People **clapperclaw** *at me all the time," shrugged the traffic cop. "The more profanity they use, the more tickets I write."*

concatenate, *v.*
(kahn-KA-tuh-NAYT)
to link together like a chain
concatenation, *n.*

concionate, *v.*
(KAHN-see-oh-NAYT)
to preach
concionator, *n.*

condescend, *v.*
(kahn-duh-SEHND)
1: to treat others as if they are inferior 2: (followed by *to*) to lower oneself to the level of an inferior; to stoop to someone's level
condescension, *n.*, **condescending,** *adj.*, **condescender,** *n.*

conflate, *v.*
(kuhn-FLAYT)
to merge or lump together
conflation, *n.*
My brother always plays with his food, **conflating** *the mashed potatoes, peas, and meatloaf into one big pile.*

cosher, *v.*
(KAH-sher)
to treat with hospitality; to pamper or spoil, particularly with regard to food

cosset, *v., n.*
(KAH-siht)
1: to pamper 2: a pet

croodle, *v.*
(KROO-duhl)
to huddle together, usually from fear or cold
"It's so nice to **croodle** *with my girlfriend by the fire at night on our camping trip. Not that I'm scared or anything. Wh-what was that?"*

croodle

dactylonomy, *n.*
(DAK-tihl-AHN-uh-mee)
the act of counting on one's fingers

defenestrate, *v.*
(dee-FEH-nuh-STRAYT)
to throw out a window
defenestration, *n.*

deoppilate, *v.*
(dih-AHP-uh-LAYT)
to remove an obstruction; to clear a passage
deoppilation, *n.*
"Could you please **deoppilate** *the hallway?" Mom asked. "Your toys seem to have barricaded your father into the bedroom."*

dephlogisticcate, *v.*
(dih-floh-JIHS-tih-KAYT)
to fireproof something

discerp, *v.*
(DIH-serp)
to tear into pieces
discerpible, *adj.*

disparage, *v.*
(dih-SPAIR-ihj)
to speak ill of someone or something; to insult or belittle
disparagement, *n.*, **disparaging,** *adj.*, **disparagingly,** *adv.*

diurnation, *n.*
(dahy-er-NAY-shuhn)
the act of sleeping during the day
diurnal, *adj.*

embellish, *v.*
(ihm-BEHL-ihsh)
to decorate something; to beautify by adding things; to ornament
embellishment, *n.*, **embellished,** *adj.*, **embellisher,** *n.*

estivate, *v.*
(EHS-tuh-vayt)
to spend the summer somewhere; to spend the summer in a state of dormancy
estivation, *n.*

embellish

etiolate, *v.*
(EE-tee-uh-LAYT)
to make weak or pale
etiolation, *n.*, **etiolated,** *adj.*

evanesce, *v.*
(eh-vuh-NEHS)
to disappear like vapor
evanescence, *n.*, **evanescent,** *adj.*

exculpate, *v.*
(EHK-skuhl-payt)
to free from blame, fault, or guilt
exculpation, *n.*, **exculpatory,** *adj.*

faffle, *v.*
(FAF-uhl)
to stammer

feriation, *n.*
(fair-ee-AY-shuhn)
the act of taking time off from work; going on holiday

festinate, *v.*
(FEHS-tuh-nayt)
to hurry
festinate, *adj.*
"I know it's not in your nature," said the impatient rabbit to the turtle, "but could you at least try to **festinate***?"*

fletcherize, *v.*
(FLEH-chuh-rahyz)
to chew food slowly and
thoroughly
"If you keep **fletcherizing**,*"*
Ross complained, "you won't
finish eating for another
two hours!"

flummox, *v.*
(FLUH-muhks)
to deeply confuse someone;
to confound
flummoxed, *adj.*

fletcherize

footle, *v.*
(FOO-tuhl)
to waste time
footler, *n.*

fulgurate, *v.*
(FUHL-gyuh-rayt)
to dart or flash like lightning
fulguration, *n.,* **fulgurant,** *adj.*

fulminate, *v.*
(FUHL-muh-nayt)
to issue a thunderous verbal attack; to explode
fulmination, *n.,* **fulminant,** *adj.*
The entire neighborhood heard my dad **fulminate**
when he saw the dent I put in the car.

gallivant, *v.*
(GAL-uh-vant)
to play and roam for fun

garbology, *n.*
(gar-BAH-luh-jee)
the study of human cultures by examining what is
thrown away as trash
garbologist, *n.*

gaum, *v.*
(gawm)
to smear with a sticky substance; to mess up something
with a sticky substance

gazump, *v.*
(guh-ZUHMP)
to rip someone off; to raise the price of something
after having accepted a lower offer

geophagy, *n.*
(jee-AHF-uh-jee)
the practice of eating dirt or clay

gesticulate, *v.*
(jeh-STIH-kyuh-layt)
to gesture
gesticulation, *n.*, **gesticulator,** *n.*, **gesticulative,** *adj.*,
gesticulatory, *adj.*, **gesticulant,** *adj.*

gormandize, *v.*
(GOR-muhn-DAHYZ)
to eat greedily

grubstake, *n.*
(GRUHB-stayk)
a loan (at the start of a business in exchange for a share of the profits)

harangue, *n.*, *v.*
(huh-RANG)
1: a written or spoken rant 2: to scold
harangued, *adj.*, **haranguer,** *n.*

hector, *v.*
(HEHK-ter)
to bully, harass, or intimidate

honeyfuggle, *v.*
(HUH-nee-FUH-guhl)
to deceive by flattery or sweet-talk; to swindle or cheat
    "How did you get the hall pass?" Stew asked.
    "I just told Mrs. Blackwell how great she looked today.
A little **honeyfuggle** *goes a long way," Ann said with a*
shrug.

hoodwink, *v.*
(HOOD-wihnk)
to deceive by trickery
hoodwinker, *n.*

impinge, *v.*
(ihm-PIHNJ)
(usually followed by *upon* or *on*)
to obstruct, hinder, or
cause interference
impingement, *n.*, **impinging,** *adj.*,
impinger, *n.*

infrigidate, *v.*
(ihn-FRIHJ-ih-dayt)
to cool something
On super hot days, Zach would
infrigidate *himself by sitting in a*
bathtub full of ice.

infrigidate

infucate, *v.*
(IHN-foo-kayt)
to stain or paint; to apply makeup

itinerant, *adj.*
(ahy-TIHN-uh-ruhnt)
traveling from place to place; alternating between
working and wandering
itinerancy, *n.*

jactitate, *v.*
(JAK-tuh-tayt)
to thrash; to toss or move violently
jactitation, *n.*

jarble, *v.*
(JAR-buhl)
to wet or muddy

jauk, *v.*
(jawk)
to dawdle
*Mikayla hated going to the dentist, so she moved as slowly as possible on the walk there. "Don't **jauk** so much," her father scolded over his shoulder. "Keep up!"*

kibitz, *v.*
(KIH-bihts)
to offer unwanted advice or unnecessary commentary
kibitzer, *n.*

lambaste, *v.*
(lam-BAYST)
to scold sharply; to berate
*When Charlie's mother caught him cheating, she **lambasted** him. "Stop that this instant, Charlie! I'm furious with you!" she cried out.*

lambaste

lament, *v.*
(luh-MEHNT)
to regret or express sorrow for something
lamentation, *n.*, **lamentable,** *adj.*, **lamenter,** *n.*

latrate, *v.*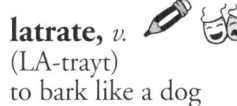
(LA-trayt)
to bark like a dog

legerdemain, *n.*
(LEH-jer-duh-MAYN)
sleight (cleverness and quickness) of hand; a show of skill or deceitful cleverness; an artful trick

logrolling, *n.*
(LAWG-roh-lihng)
offering a favor in exchange for a favor, especially in politics; back-scratching
logroll, *v.*

lollygag, *v.*
(LAH-lee-gag)
to move slowly or dawdle

madefy, *v.*
(MAD-ih-fahy)
to moisten
A terrible sound came from Bob's clarinet. "You must **madefy** *your lips first!" his teacher explained. After giving them a lick, he blew again, and a much less terrible sound came out.*

maffick, *v.*
(MA-fihk)
to celebrate with boisterous and silly behavior

manducate, *v.*
(MAN-dyoo-kayt)
to chew or eat

moil, *v.*
(MOY-uhl)
to work slavishly
moiling, *adj.,* **moiler,** *n.*

mollify, *v.*
(MAH-luh-fahy)
to soothe or calm
mollification, *n.,* **mollifiable,** *adj.,* **mollifier,** *n.,*
mollifyingly, *adv.*

mudslinging, *n.*
(MUHD-slihng-ihng)
the use of insults and innuendo to discredit an opponent
mudslinger, *n.*

mulligan, *n.*
(MUHL-ih-guhn)
a second shot allowed when the first shot is hopelessly messed up; a do-over

nictitate, *v.*
(NIHK-tuh-tayt)
to wink or blink

nidificate, *v.*
(NIHD-uh-fuh-kayt)
to build a nest
nidification, *n.*

obfuscate, *v.*
(AHB-fuh-skayt)
to hide in darkness; to confuse or muddle
an issue
obfuscation, *n.*

obnubilate, *v.*
(ahb-NOO-buh-layt)
to cloud over; to obscure
obnubilation, *n.*

omphaloskepsis

omphaloskepsis, *n.*
(AHM-fa-loh-SKEHP-suss)
 contemplation of one's belly button
*"What are you doing?" she asked as he
stared at his navel.*
 *"**Omphaloskepsis**," he explained.
"It helps me think … and, look, I found
another piece of lint!"*

osculate, *v.*
(AHS-kyuh-layt)
to kiss
osculation, *n.*, **osculatory,** *adj.*

pagophagia, *n.*
(PAH-guh-FAY-jee-uh)
compulsive eating of ice
pagophagic, *adj.*

patronize, *v.*
(PAY-truh-nahyz)
to behave in an offensively superior manner toward
someone; to condescend
patronizing, *adj.*, **patronizer,** *n.*, **patronizingly,** *adv.*

peenge, *v.*
(peenj)
to complain

perambulate, *v.*
(puh-RAM-byuh-layt)
to walk or stroll
perambulatory, *adj.*, **perambulation,** *n.*,
perambulator, *n.*

peregrinate, *v.*
(PER-uh-gruh-nayt)
to travel, especially on foot
peregrination, *n.*

periclitate, *v.*
(puh-RIHK-luh-tayt)
to endanger

peripatetic, *adj.*
(PAIR-uh-puh-TEH-tihk)
walking or traveling about

peristerophily, *n.*
(per-IH-ster-AH-fuh-lee)
the training of pigeons
   "**Peristerophily** *is a noble hobby,"
declared Mr. Smith. "Homing pigeons
have received medals for their heroic
actions during wartime."
   "True," said his neighbor. "But I still
doubt you'll ever teach one to jump
through a hoop."*

peristerophily

pernoctation, *n.*
(per-nahk-TAY-shuhn)
the act of spending an entire night doing something;
an all-night vigil

pogonotomy, *n.*
(poh-guh-NAH-tuh-mee)
the cutting of a beard

pogonotrophy, *n.*
(poh-guh-NAH-truh-fee)
the growing of a beard; beardedness

pontificate, *v.*
(pahn-TIH-fuh-kayt)
to speak at length in a patronizing or pompous manner
pontification, *n.*, **pontificator,** *n.*

prestidigitation, *n.*
(PREHS-tuh-dih-juh-TAY-shuhn)
cleverness and quickness of the hands, usually for means
of deception or trickery
prestidigitator, *n.*

prevaricate, *v.*
(prih-VAIR-uh-kayt)
to deliberately mislead by withholding information
or by being unclear; to lie
prevarication, *n.*

prink, *v.*
(preenk)
to get decked out; to fuss over one's appearance
prinker, *n.*
Audra's older sister loved to **prink***. She would spend hours
locked in her room, putting on clothes and makeup, even if
she had nowhere to go, which was most of the time.*

proliferate, *v.*
(proh-LIHF-uh-rayt)
to spread or grow rapidly
proliferation, *n.*, **proliferative,** *adj.*, **proliferator,** *n.*

pugilism, *n.*
(PYOO-juh-lih-zuhm)
the sport of boxing
pugilist, *n.*, **pugilistic,** *adj.*

"Step into the ring," he said,
tossing a set of gloves to his
brother. "Let's go a few rounds."
"That's not a ring, it's my
living room," his mom said.

pugilism

"And there'll be no **pugilism** *in the house!"*

revile, *v.*
(rih-VAHYL)
to speak to someone in an abusive manner;
to rail against someone

rhonchisonant  *adj.*
(rahn-KIH-suh-nuhnt)
making a snorting sound

rubricate, *v.*
(ROO-brih-kayt)
to mark with red
rubrication, *n.*

sanction, *v.*
(SANGK-shuhn)
to approve, authorize, or allow
sanctionable, *adj.*

segue, *v.*, *n.*
(SEHG-way)
1: to make an uninterrupted transition or change; to lead into something else 2: a transition without interruption

skedaddle, 🖉
(skih-DA-duhl)
to leave quickly
skedaddler, *n.*

snarf, *v.* 🎭
(snarf)
to eat or drink rapidly

spoliate, *v.*
(SPOH-lee-ayt)
to plunder, ruin, or rob

steganography, *n.*
(STEHG-uh-NAH-gruh-fee)
the art of creating and
transmitting coded messages
steganographist, *n.*,
steganographic, *adj.*
Just to be safe, Megan used
steganography *when she*
passed a note to Sara about the boy she liked.

steganography

tergiversate, *v.*
(ter-JIH-ver-sayt)
to speak or act evasively; to be intentionally unclear in an attempt to mislead
tergiversation, *n.*

titivate, *v.*
(TIH-tuh-vayt)
to spruce up or neaten up
titivation, *n.*

vellicate, *v.*
(VEHL-uh-kayt)
to slightly irritate a part of the body and cause it to twitch or tickle

venerate, *v.*
(VEHN-uh-rayt)
to treat with respect or reverence
venerable, *adj.*

verbigerate, *v.*
(ver-BIH-juh-rayt)
to obsessively repeat nonsense
verbigeration, *n.*, **verbigerative,** *adj.*

vilify, *v.*
(VIH-luh-fahy)
to portray someone in a negative light; to slander
vilification, *n.*, **vilifier,** *n.*

vindicate, *v.*
(VIHN-dih-kayt)
to clear or free of accusation or blame
vindication, *n.*, **vindicated,** *adj.*, **vindicator,** *n.*

vitiate, *v.*
(VIH-shee-ayt)
to lower the quality of something; to corrupt; to spoil or ruin
vitiation, *n.*

vivify, *v.*
(VIH-vuh-fahy)
to make something livelier or more spirited
vivification, *n.*, **vivific,** *adj.*, **vivifier,** *n.*

woolgathering, *n.*
(WOOL-ga-ther-rihng)
indulgence in idle daydreaming
woolgather, *v.*, **woolgatherer,** *n.*
After the new boy said hello to her in class, Dena sat with her eyes glazed over until the teacher shrieked, "Dena! Stop that **woolgathering** *and pay attention!"*

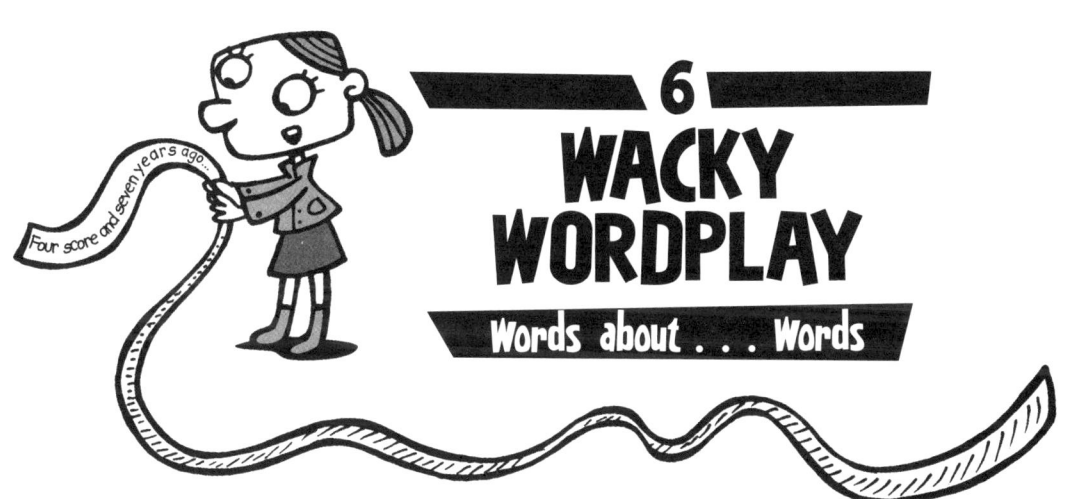

6
WACKY WORDPLAY
Words about . . . . Words

abecedarian, *adj., n.*
(AY-bee-see-DER-ee-uhn)
1: of or relating to the alphabet 2: a beginner

adoxography, *n.*
(ay-dahks-AH-gruh-fee)
skilled writing about a subject of no importance

alliteration, *n.*
(uh-LIH-tuh-RAY-shuhn)
repetition of the same consonant sounds at the
beginning of words; tongue twisters usually provide
examples of alliteration, e.g., *Peter Piper picked a peck of
pickled peppers.*
alliterative, *adj.*

altiloquent, *adj.*
(al-TIH-loh-kwuhnt)
pompous in speech
altiloquence, *n.*

amphigory, *n.*
(am-fuh-GOR-ee)
a nonsense piece of writing
amphigoric, *adj.*

anopisthograph, *n.*
(AN-uh-PIHS-thuh-GRAF)
a book with writing on only one side of each page; a
piece of paper with writing on only one side
anopisthographic, *adj.*

antonomasia, *n.*
(AN-tuh-nuh-MAY-zhuh)
the use of a descriptive name or designation as a name
antonomastic, *adj.*

aposiopesis, *n.*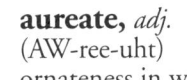
(AP-uh-SAHY-uh-PEE-suss)
the breaking off in the middle of speaking
a thought

aptronym, *n.*
(AP-truh-nihm)
a fitting name

aureate, *adj.*
(AW-ree-uht)
ornateness in writing or speaking

bafflegab, *n.* ✏
(BA-fuhl-gab)
incomprehensible speech; nonsense
I asked my little brother how his trick-or-treating went, but his mouth was so full of candy that whatever he said just sounded like **bafflegab**.

bafflegab

CHAPTER

6

battology, *n.*
(ba-TAWL-uh-jee)
wearisome repetition of words in speech or writing
battologize, *v.*

bibliophile, *n.*
(BIH-blee-uh-fahyl)
a lover of books
bibliophilic, *adj.*, **bibliophilism,** *n.*

billingsgate, *n.*
(BIHL-ihngz-gayt)
foul, abusive language

blatteroon, *n.*
(BLA-tuh-roon)
one who brags or talks incessantly

bowdlerize, *v.*
(BOHD-luh-rahyz)
to purge a written work of objectionable material; to simplify or distort a written work
bowdlerization, *n.*

breviloquent, *v.*
(brehv-IH-loh-kwuhnt)
brief in speech
breviloquence, *n.*

cacoepy, *n.*
(kak-OH-uh-pee)
incorrect pronunciation
cacoepistic, *adj.*

circumlocution, *n.*
(SER-kuhm-loh-KYOO-shuhn)
the use of many words to express an idea or concept
that could easily be expressed by a few
circumlocutory, *adj.*

codswallop, *n.*
(KAHDZ-wahl-uhp)
nonsense

cognomen, *n.*
(kahg-NOH-muhn)
a family name or surname
cognominal, *adj.*

colloquialism, *n.*
(kuh-LOH-kwee-uh-LIH-zuhm)
informal language
colloquial, *adj.*

cruciverbalist, *n.*
(KROO-suh-VER-buh-lihst)
one who loves to solve or create crossword puzzles

eisegesis, *n.*
(AHY-suh-JEE-suss)
a personal interpretation of a book or other work

epeolatry, *n.*
(EH-pee-AH-luh-tree)
the worship of words
epeolatrous, *adj.*
His **epeolatry** *was so extreme
that whenever he made a solemn
promise, he swore on a stack of
dictionaries instead of bibles!*

eponym, *n.*
(EH-puh-nihm)
a word derived from a person's name
eponymous, *adj.*

eroteme, *n.*
(ER-uh-teem)
the "?" symbol used in writing

euphemism, *n.*
(YOO-fuh-mih-zuhm)
a nicer way to say something
euphemistic, *adj.*

epeolatry

factoid, *n.*
(FAK-toyd)
a trivial fact

falderal, *n.*
(FAHL-duh-rahl)
foolish talk; nonsense
   "I'll never be big enough to scare the other dinosaurs,"
complained the young T. Rex.
   *"That's **falderal**," his mother responded. "Trust me,*
when you grow up, you'll be very scary."

flapdoodle, *n.*
(FLAP-doo-duhl)
nonsense; foolish talk

florid, *adj.*
(FLOR-ihd)
elaborateness or floweriness in speech or writing
floridity, *n.*, **floridly,** *adv.*, **floridness,** *n.*

garrulous, *adj.*
(GAIR-uh-luss)
extremely talkative
garrulity, *n.*, **garrulously,** *adv.*, **garrulousness,** *n.*

glottology, *n.*
(glah-TAH-luh-jee)
the science of languages
glottologist, *n.*

gobbledygook, *n.*
(GAH-buhl-dee-GOOK)
incomprehensible speech; nonsense

grammaticaster, *n.*
(gruh-MAT-ih-KAS-ter)
a person who is petty about proper grammar

grandiloquence, *n.*
(gran-DIH-luh-kwehns)
speech or expression filled with fancy, haughty language
grandiloquent, *adj.*, **grandiloquently,** *adv.*

graphophobia, *n.*
(GRAF-uh-FOH-bee-uh)
fear of writing or of writings
graphophobe, *n.*, **graphophobic,** *adj.*

heterography, *n.*
(heht-er-AH-gruh-fee)
misspellings
heterographic, *adj.*, **heterographical,** *adj.*

heterophemy, *n.*
(HEHT-uh-ruh-FEE-mee)
the accidental use of words one did not intend to use
heterophemize, *v.*

hypocorism

hypocorism, *n.*
(hahy-puh-KOR-ih-zuhm)
a pet name
hypocoristic, *adj.*

inaniloquent, *adj.*
(ih-nay-NIHL-oh-kwuhnt)
given to inane speech

karmadharaya, *n.*
(kar-muh-DAR-ee-uh)
a compound word in which the first half is an adjective
that describes the second half, which is a noun (e.g.,
blueberry or gentleman)

lethologica, *n.*
(lee-thoh-LAH-jih-kuh)
the inability to remember the right word for something
lethological, *adj.*

lexicon, *n.*
(LEHK-sih-kahn)
a stock of terms used in a particular profession, style, or
subject; lingo

lexiconophilia, *n.*
(LEHK-sih-KAH-noh-FEEL-yuh)
love of dictionaries and word books
lexiconophiliac, *n.*

lexiphanicism, *n.*
(LEHK-sih-FAN-ih-sih-zuhm)
use of pretentious, showy words

logodaedaly, *n.*
(LOH-guh-DEE-duh-lee)
the clever creation of new words; the clever use of words

logomachy, *n.*
(luh-GAH-muh-kee)
a dispute over words

logomaniac, *n.*
(LOH-guh-MAY-nee-ak)
a person obsessed with words
logomania, *n.*

logorrhea, *n.*
(loh-guh-REE-uh)
compulsive, repetitive speech
logorrheic, *adj.*

loquacious, *adj.*
(loh-KWAY-shuss)
very talkative
loquaciously, *adv.*, **loquaciousness,** *n.*, **loquacity,** *n.*

magniloquent, *adj.*
(mag-NIHL-uh-kwuhnt)
lofty or grandiose in speech or expression
magniloquence, *n.*, **magniloquently,** *adv.*

malapropism, *n.*
(MA-luh-PRAH-pih-zuhm)
misuse of a word, especially by confusion with a
similar word
malaprop, *n.*, **malapropian,** *adj.*, **malapropist,** *n.*

maledicent, *adj.*
(mal-ih-DIH-suhnt)
speaking meanly or slanderously about someone
maledicency, *n.*

marginalia, *n.*
(MAR-juh-NAY-lee-uh)
notes written in the margins of a page
*Monica was furious. When Richard returned the book he
had borrowed, the pages were filled with* **marginalia***.*
"Who said you could write in my book?" she demanded.
*"I thought you might be
interested in my opinion,"
replied Richard.*
*"Well, 'She's sooooo cute!'
and 'This part is dumb!' are
not my idea of razor-sharp
commentary."*

Note to self:
Don't write in other
people's books

marginalia

melliloquent, *adj.*
(meh-LIH-loh-kwuhnt)
smooth in speech
melliloquence, *n.*

mondegreen, *n.*
(MAHN-duh-green)
a word or phrase that has been misheard or misinterpreted

moniker, *n.*
(MAH-nih-ker)
a nickname
Ernest the Elephant decided he needed a **moniker***. "From now on," he said, "please call me 'Big E.'"*

neologism, *n.*
(nee-AH-luh-jih-zuhm)
a new word, usage, or expression
neologistic, *adj.*

nomenclature, *n.*
(NOH-muhn-KLAY-cher)
a system of names used in an art or science
nomenclatural, *adj.*

onomatopoeia, *n.*
(AH-nuh-MAH-tuh-PEE-uh)
a word meant to imitate sound (e.g., meow; plop; splash)
onomatopoetic, *adj.*,
onomatopoetically, *adv.*

onomatopoeia

oxymoron, *n.*
(AHK-see-MOR-ahn)
a statement that seems to contradict itself; a combination of contradictory words (e.g., pretty ugly; loud silence)
oxymoronic, *adj.*, **oxymoronically,** *adv.*

palindrome, *n.*
(PA-luhn-drohm)
a word, verse, phrase, or sentence that reads the same backward and forward (e.g., "Madam, I'm Adam;" "Hannah;" "Mom")
palindromic, *adj.*, **palindromist,** *n.*
 "Madam, I'm Adam," said Otis.
 "Ah, so you're doing **palindromes** *again," she replied.*
"Well, I have one for you, too: 'Sit on a potato pan, Otis!'"

paradiorthosis, *n.*
(pah-ruh-DAHY-or-thoh-sis)
the introduction of errors into a text while attempting to correct it; an incorrect correction

paronomasia, *n.*
(PAIR-uh-noh-MAY-zhuh)
a pun; a play on words

pejorative, *n.*, *adj.*
(pih-JOR-uh-tihv)
1: a word or phrase that abuses or disparages someone; an abusive comment 2: disparaging
pejoratively, *adv.*

persiflage, *n.*
(PER-sih-flahj)
light-hearted discussion

poetaster, *n.*
(POH-uh-TAS-ter)
a writer of bad poetry

poppycock, *n.*
(PAH-pee-kahk)
nonsense

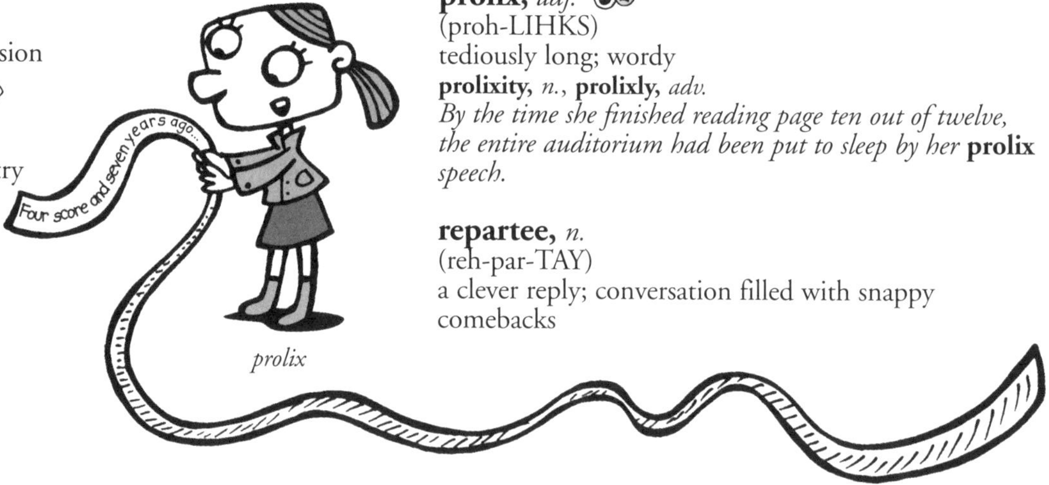

prolix, *adj.*
(proh-LIHKS)
tediously long; wordy
prolixity, *n.*, **prolixly,** *adv.*
By the time she finished reading page ten out of twelve, the entire auditorium had been put to sleep by her **prolix** *speech.*

repartee, *n.*
(reh-par-TAY)
a clever reply; conversation filled with snappy comebacks

Four score and seven years ago...

prolix

rhetoric, *n.*
(REH-ter-ihk)
persuasive language
rhetorical, *adj.*, **rhetorically,** *adv.*

sesquipedalian, *adj.*
(SEHS-kwuh-puh-DAYL-yuhn)
given to the use of long words

sockdolager, *n.*
(sahk-DAHL-uh-jer)
a deciding remark or knockdown blow

tachyphasia, *n.*
(tahk-ee-FAY-zhuh)
extremely rapid speech

verbose, *adj.*
(ver-BOHS)
wordy; lengthy
verbosely, *adv.*, **verboseness,** *n.*, **verbosity,** *n.*

vernacular, *n.*
(ver-NAK-yuh-ler)
the nonstandard language of a particular area or group
vernacularly, *adv.*

INDEX OF WORDS

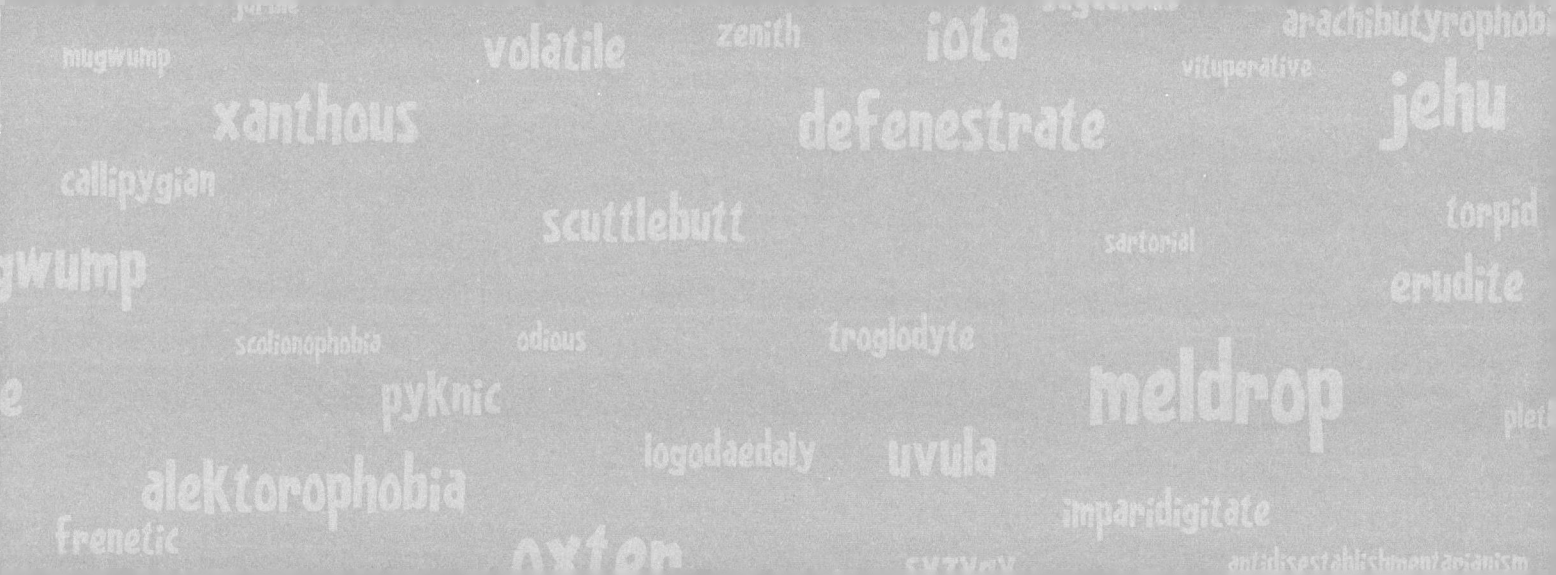

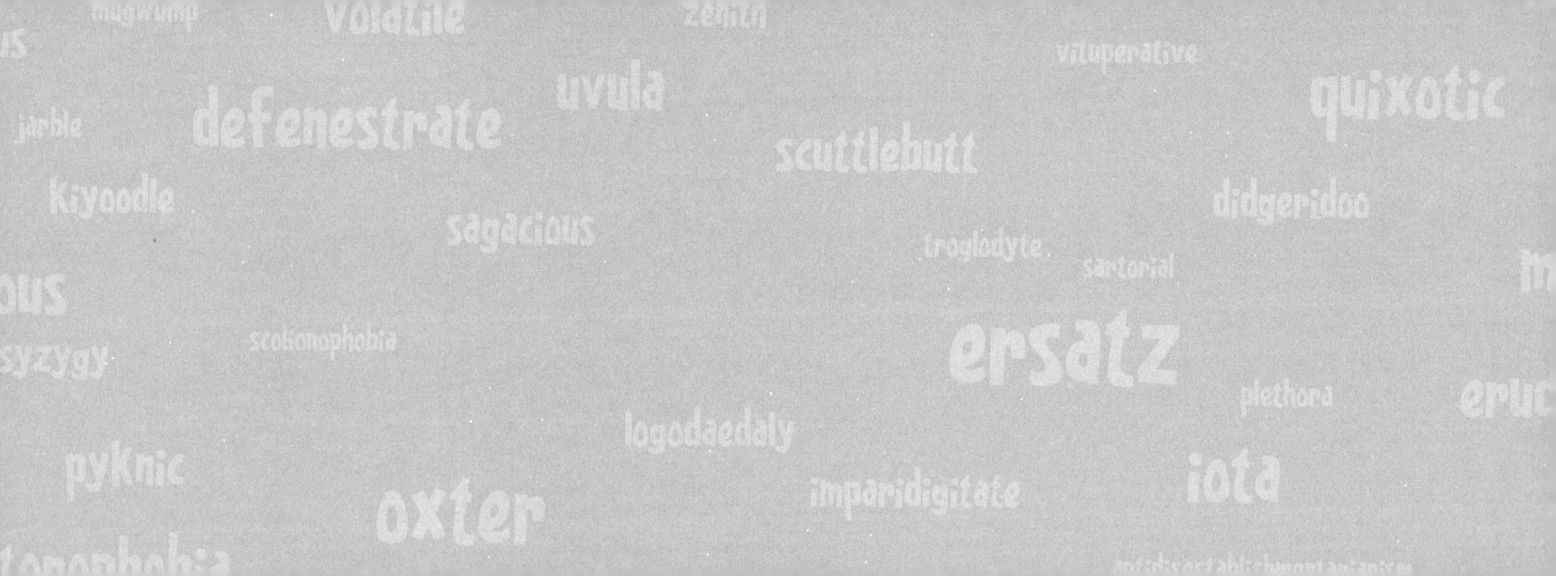